The AI Dilemma
Humanity at the Crossroads

Introduction: The Age of AI and the Human Dilemma

Artificial Intelligence (AI) has become one of the most powerful and transformative forces in modern society. Its impact is already evident in nearly every aspect of human life, from healthcare and finance to education, entertainment, and national security. AI-powered algorithms make real-time decisions that affect billions of people daily, whether by recommending personalized content, optimizing supply chains, or diagnosing diseases. These advancements have led to groundbreaking efficiencies, but they have also introduced significant risks and ethical challenges. The rise of AI is not merely a technological evolution; it is a defining moment in human history—one that presents an unavoidable dilemma: Will AI serve as a force for good, enhancing human potential and solving global challenges, or will it lead to a future where humanity is overshadowed by machines that we can no longer control?

As AI progresses, it forces us to confront fundamental questions about the nature of intelligence, consciousness, and control. Will AI surpass human intelligence, and if so, what are the consequences? Can we create ethical safeguards to ensure AI systems align with human values, or will they inherit and amplify the biases present in the data they are trained on? How will AI reshape economies, displacing entire industries while creating new ones? Perhaps most importantly, does AI serve humanity, or is it becoming an entity with its own objectives, driven by the corporations and governments that deploy it? These questions define what can be called the AI dilemma, a moment of reckoning where humanity must make critical decisions about the future of artificial intelligence before it is too late.

The rapid advancement of AI is largely fueled by exponential increases in computing power, the availability of massive datasets, and the refinement of deep learning algorithms. Just a few decades ago, AI was limited to rule-based systems with minimal learning capabilities. Today, AI systems can generate realistic human-like text, produce deepfake videos indistinguishable from reality, and even outperform human professionals in complex domains such as medical diagnostics and legal analysis. Machines have already beaten the world's best chess players, mastered intricate strategic games like Go, and are now capable of composing music, writing essays, and creating art. What was once a field of academic curiosity has become an essential pillar of modern civilization, one that continues to expand into new territories.

With these advancements come significant risks. Algorithmic bias has been well-documented, leading to unfair outcomes in hiring, policing, and lending decisions. AI-powered surveillance raises concerns about privacy, individual freedoms, and authoritarian control. The automation of jobs threatens to create mass unemployment and widen economic inequality, leaving millions without viable career paths. The rise of autonomous weapons introduces new threats to global security, where AI-driven warfare could eliminate human oversight from the decision-making process. And perhaps the most concerning possibility of all is the emergence of artificial general intelligence (AGI)—a form of AI that can think, learn, and operate independently, potentially surpassing human intelligence and operating beyond our control.

At this moment in time, humanity is at a crossroads. One path leads to a future where AI is developed responsibly, governed by ethical frameworks that prioritize human dignity, fairness, and sustainability. This scenario envisions AI as a tool that augments human intelligence, solves pressing global issues, and fosters economic and social prosperity. The other path, however, leads to an uncontrolled AI revolution—one where technological advancements outpace our ability to regulate them, resulting in societal upheaval, loss of privacy, increased inequality, and potentially even existential threats. Which direction we take will depend on the decisions we make today, both as individuals and as a collective society.

This book aims to explore the complexities of the AI dilemma by examining both its extraordinary potential and its profound risks. It will delve into the history of AI, the economic and ethical challenges it presents, and the critical role governments, corporations, and individuals must play in shaping its trajectory. Through real-world examples, expert insights, and in-depth analysis, this book will navigate the competing narratives about AI's future—whether it will be humanity's greatest achievement or its ultimate downfall. At the heart of this discussion lies a central question: Do we control AI, or is AI beginning to control us? The answer to this question will define the course of human civilization for generations to come.

Chapter 1
The Genesis of Artificial Intelligence

Artificial Intelligence (AI) is often perceived as a modern marvel, yet its origins trace back to the early philosophical inquiries about intelligence and the mechanization of human thought. The idea that machines could mimic human reasoning has fascinated scientists, mathematicians, and visionaries for centuries. From ancient automatons designed to perform simple tasks to the sophisticated neural networks of today, AI has evolved through a series of breakthroughs, each pushing the boundaries of what machines can achieve. The journey of AI is not just a story of technological innovation—it is a testament to humanity's relentless pursuit of understanding intelligence itself.

The genesis of AI can be understood as an intersection of various disciplines, including mathematics, logic, psychology, and engineering. Early computational theories laid the groundwork for the field, with figures like Alan Turing proposing the possibility of machines that could simulate human intelligence. Turing's famous 1950 paper, Computing Machinery and Intelligence, posed the now-iconic question: "Can machines think?" He introduced the Turing Test, a criterion for determining whether a machine could exhibit intelligent behavior indistinguishable from that of a human. His work, along with contributions from other pioneers, set the stage for AI's development as an academic and technological field.

The official birth of AI as a scientific discipline is often traced back to the Dartmouth Conference of 1956, where John McCarthy, Marvin Minsky, Nathaniel Rochester, and Claude Shannon convened to discuss the possibility of creating machines that could simulate human intelligence. McCarthy coined the term "artificial intelligence" to define the field, and the conference marked the beginning of AI research as a distinct area of study. The optimism of the early researchers was boundless—they believed that within a few decades, AI systems would rival human cognition. However, they soon encountered significant challenges, as the computing power and data required to support advanced AI were still decades away.

In its early years, AI research focused on rule-based systems, symbolic reasoning, and expert systems designed to mimic human decision-making in specific domains. Programs such as ELIZA, an early natural language processing chatbot developed in the 1960s, demonstrated how machines could simulate human-like interactions, though without genuine understanding. The 1970s and 1980s saw setbacks known as "AI winters," periods in which enthusiasm and funding for AI declined due to the slow progress and overpromises that could not be fulfilled. Yet, even during these difficult times, foundational work was being laid for future advancements.

The resurgence of AI in the late 20th and early 21st centuries was fueled by several key developments: exponential growth in computational power, the rise of machine learning, and the availability of vast amounts of digital data. The transition from rule-based programming to data-driven learning marked a pivotal shift. Instead of programming explicit rules, AI systems began to learn patterns from data, leading to the emergence of deep learning and neural networks. This shift has propelled AI to new heights, enabling it to recognize images, process natural language, and even defeat human champions in games like chess and Go.

As we look at the history of AI, it is clear that each breakthrough has been both a technological advancement and a philosophical challenge. The quest to build intelligent machines raises profound questions about what it means to be human, the nature of intelligence, and the limits of artificial systems. While AI has made extraordinary progress, its full potential—and its ultimate consequences—remain uncertain. The genesis of AI is not just a story of machines learning to think; it is a reflection of humanity's deep-seated desire to understand and replicate intelligence itself.

From Mechanical Computation to Machine Learning

The evolution of artificial intelligence (AI) from mechanical computation to machine learning is a fascinating journey that highlights humanity's pursuit of creating intelligent systems. This transformation did not happen overnight; it was the result of centuries of innovation in mathematics, logic, and computing. From the earliest mechanical devices designed to perform calculations to today's sophisticated machine learning models, each step has brought us closer to the goal of building intelligent machines capable of learning, reasoning, and making decisions independently.

The foundation of AI can be traced back to mechanical computation, where early inventors sought to create machines that could assist with mathematical calculations. One of the most notable figures in this era was Blaise Pascal, who, in the 17th century, invented the Pascaline, a mechanical calculator capable of performing basic arithmetic operations. Following Pascal, the German mathematician Gottfried Wilhelm Leibniz improved upon this design by developing the stepped reckoner, which could multiply and divide. These early mechanical devices laid the groundwork for the idea that machines could be programmed to perform logical operations.

The 19th century saw further advancements with Charles Babbage's design of the Analytical Engine, a mechanical general-purpose computing device that featured concepts still used in modern computers, such as memory storage and sequential control. Although Babbage never completed a working model, his vision inspired future generations of computer scientists. Ada Lovelace, often credited as the first computer programmer, recognized that the Analytical Engine could go beyond mere calculations—it could be programmed to follow instructions and even create patterns. This insight foreshadowed the core idea behind AI: machines capable of executing complex, human-like tasks through predefined rules and instructions.

The 20th century marked a pivotal shift from mechanical computation to electronic computing. Alan Turing, a British mathematician and logician, played a crucial role in this transition. His theoretical work laid the foundation for modern computing and AI. In 1936, he introduced the concept of the Turing Machine, a hypothetical device capable of executing any computable function given the right set of instructions. This concept became the blueprint for the first general-purpose computers. Turing's work during World War II, particularly in breaking the German Enigma code using computational methods, demonstrated the potential of machines to solve complex problems.

As computers became more powerful, researchers began exploring ways to create systems that could simulate human intelligence. Early AI research focused on rule-based systems and symbolic reasoning, where programmers explicitly defined logical rules for machines to follow. However, these approaches had limitations—rule-based AI required extensive manual coding and struggled with tasks involving ambiguity or large datasets. It became clear that for AI to truly advance, machines needed the ability to learn from data rather than rely solely on predefined rules.

This realization led to the birth of machine learning, a subfield of AI that focuses on developing algorithms capable of identifying patterns and improving their performance over time. Instead of being explicitly programmed with rules, machine learning models are trained on large datasets, allowing them to recognize trends, make predictions, and adapt to new information. This shift was made possible by the exponential growth in computing power, the availability of vast amounts of digital data, and advancements in statistical methods.

Neural networks, inspired by the structure of the human brain, became a game-changer in AI research. Although the concept was introduced in the 1950s, it wasn't until the rise of deep learning in the 21st century that neural networks achieved remarkable breakthroughs. Deep learning models, powered by massive datasets and high-performance computing, now enable AI to perform complex tasks such as natural language processing, image recognition, and even autonomous decision-making.

The transition from mechanical computation to machine learning represents a fundamental shift in how we approach AI. It marks the evolution from rigid, rule-based systems to dynamic, adaptive models that can learn and evolve. As machine learning continues to advance, it raises profound questions about the future of AI—its capabilities, its ethical implications, and its role in shaping the future of humanity.

Defining the Crossroads: Progress vs. Peril

Humanity stands at a critical crossroads in the evolution of artificial intelligence (AI). The rapid advancements in AI technology have created unprecedented opportunities for progress while simultaneously introducing profound risks that could reshape society in ways we are not yet prepared to handle. This intersection—where AI's potential for innovation collides with its potential for disruption—is the defining dilemma of our time. Will AI be the driving force behind a golden age of human prosperity, or will it spiral out of control, creating new forms of inequality, manipulation, and even existential threats? The choices we make today will determine whether AI remains a tool for human empowerment or becomes a force that endangers our autonomy, security, and ethics.

The promise of AI is undeniable. Already, machine learning models are transforming industries, from healthcare and education to finance and transportation. AI-driven algorithms are diagnosing diseases more accurately than human doctors, optimizing complex logistical networks, and even accelerating scientific research in ways never before possible. Automation is increasing efficiency and reducing human error, leading to safer and more productive workplaces. In creative fields, AI-generated art, music, and literature are pushing the boundaries of what machines can accomplish. AI has the potential to enhance nearly every aspect of human life, solving some of our most pressing challenges, such as climate change, resource management, and poverty alleviation.

However, alongside these promises lies the peril of AI's unchecked development. One of the most immediate concerns is job displacement. Automation threatens to replace millions of workers, leading to economic instability and widening the gap between the wealthy and the working class. Traditional industries may be rendered obsolete, leaving entire communities struggling to adapt. The challenge is not just about job loss but about redefining the role of human labor in an AI-driven economy.

Beyond economics, AI also raises serious ethical concerns. Algorithmic bias has already been observed in critical areas like hiring, policing, and financial lending, where AI systems have demonstrated discrimination based on race, gender, and socio-economic status. The very data that trains AI can reinforce societal inequalities, making AI decisions inherently flawed. If left unregulated, these biases could become deeply embedded in the systems that govern our lives, perpetuating injustice on a massive scale.

Privacy is another pressing issue. Governments and corporations are increasingly using AI for mass surveillance, tracking individuals' behaviors, and predicting actions before they happen. While these technologies can be used for public safety, they also pose the risk of eroding civil liberties, enabling authoritarian control, and limiting personal freedoms. The trade-off between security and privacy has never been more contentious, and AI sits at the heart of this debate.

Perhaps the most existential risk is the rise of artificial general intelligence (AGI)—AI that can think, learn, and make decisions without human intervention. While AGI remains theoretical, its potential consequences are staggering. If AI surpasses human intelligence and operates beyond our control, it could make decisions that are not aligned with human values or interests. Whether intentionally or unintentionally, such an AI could reshape the world in ways that are impossible to predict.

At this crucial juncture, the choices we make will define the future of AI and, consequently, the future of humanity. Governments, researchers, and industry leaders must work together to establish ethical guidelines, enforce regulations, and ensure AI's development aligns with human values. The challenge is to strike a balance between fostering innovation and preventing catastrophic risks. AI is not inherently good or evil—it is a tool, and its impact will depend on how it is designed, implemented, and governed.

The AI crossroads is not just a technological debate; it is a moral and philosophical one. Are we building AI to serve humanity, or are we surrendering control to it? The path we choose will determine whether AI becomes a beacon of progress or a harbinger of peril. The time to decide is now.

AI in Everyday Life: A Silent Revolution

Artificial Intelligence (AI) has quietly become an inseparable part of daily life, revolutionizing the way we interact with technology, businesses, and even one another. While many still associate AI with futuristic robots or complex scientific research, the reality is that AI operates behind the scenes in ways most people do not even realize. From personalized recommendations on streaming services to virtual assistants like Siri and Alexa, AI is seamlessly woven into the fabric of modern life. This silent revolution is reshaping industries, streamlining daily tasks, and transforming human experiences in profound ways.

One of the most visible applications of AI is in consumer technology. Smartphones, smart speakers, and home automation systems rely on AI-powered virtual assistants to help users set reminders, check the weather, or control household appliances with voice commands. These systems continuously learn from user behavior, becoming more accurate and intuitive over time. AI-driven recommendation engines in streaming services like Netflix, YouTube, and Spotify analyze viewing and listening habits to suggest content tailored to individual preferences. Similarly, e-commerce platforms like Amazon use AI to personalize shopping experiences, predicting what customers might want based on their browsing history and purchase patterns.

AI is also making significant advancements in healthcare, improving both diagnosis and treatment. AI-powered tools can analyze medical images with remarkable precision, detecting conditions such as cancer and heart disease earlier than human doctors in some cases. Wearable health devices, such as smartwatches and fitness trackers, use AI to monitor heart rates, sleep patterns, and physical activity, providing real-time health insights and even alerting users to potential medical issues. Telemedicine platforms leverage AI to offer virtual consultations, making healthcare more accessible, especially in remote areas.

In transportation, AI is revolutionizing mobility through navigation systems, traffic management, and autonomous vehicles. Apps like Google Maps and Waze use AI to analyze real-time traffic conditions, providing optimal routes to drivers. AI-powered ride-sharing services like Uber and Lyft predict demand, optimize pricing, and match drivers with passengers efficiently. Meanwhile, self-driving cars, once considered science fiction, are becoming a reality as companies like Tesla, Waymo, and others develop autonomous driving technology. These vehicles use AI to process vast amounts of sensor data, enabling them to navigate roads, detect obstacles, and make driving decisions with minimal human intervention.

AI's impact extends to financial services, where it enhances security and efficiency. Banks and payment processors use AI algorithms to detect fraudulent transactions in real-time, identifying suspicious activity and protecting customers from cyber threats. AI-driven chatbots assist customers with banking inquiries, reducing wait times and improving customer service. Investment firms leverage AI-powered analytics to predict market trends, helping traders and investors make more informed decisions.

Even in education, AI is playing a crucial role in transforming learning experiences. Intelligent tutoring systems adapt to students' individual learning styles, providing personalized feedback and recommendations. AI-powered language translation tools break down language barriers, making education more accessible to people worldwide. Automated grading systems help teachers evaluate assignments more efficiently, allowing them to focus on providing deeper insights and guidance to students.

Despite these remarkable advancements, the integration of AI into everyday life also raises concerns about privacy, data security, and ethical implications. AI systems collect vast amounts of personal data to improve their performance, but this data must be handled responsibly to prevent misuse. The reliance on AI also raises questions about job displacement, as automation continues to replace traditional roles in various industries. As AI's presence in daily life continues to grow, it is essential to strike a balance between innovation and ethical considerations.

The silent revolution of AI is reshaping society in ways both seen and unseen. Whether through personalized recommendations, smarter healthcare solutions, or safer transportation, AI enhances efficiency, convenience, and decision-making across countless domains. As this technology evolves, its impact will only deepen, making it more important than ever to ensure that AI development aligns with human values and benefits all of society.

The First Warning Signs: When AI Goes Wrong

Artificial Intelligence (AI) has undoubtedly transformed industries, improved efficiencies, and enhanced human capabilities. However, as AI systems become more powerful and integrated into society, we have begun to see warning signs of its unintended consequences. While AI is designed to operate based on logic, data, and algorithms, it does not possess human morality or ethical reasoning. As a result, when AI goes wrong, the consequences can range from minor inconveniences to severe societal harm. From algorithmic biases and misinformation to job displacement and security threats, the risks associated with AI have become increasingly evident. Recognizing these warning signs early is crucial to ensuring that AI remains a force for good rather than a tool of destruction.

One of the most alarming issues with AI is algorithmic bias and discrimination. AI systems are trained on large datasets, but if these datasets contain biases, the AI will inevitably learn and amplify them. Several high-profile cases have revealed the dangers of biased AI decision-making. For example, AI-driven hiring tools have been found to discriminate against women and minority candidates because they were trained on historical hiring data that favored male applicants. Similarly, facial recognition technology has shown higher error rates when identifying people of color, leading to wrongful arrests and ethical concerns over racial profiling. These biases are not intentional but are the result of flawed data and a lack of oversight in

AI development. Without proper safeguards, AI can perpetuate and even worsen social inequalities.

Another major concern is AI-generated misinformation and deepfakes. The rise of AI-powered content creation has made it easier than ever to generate fake news, manipulate social media trends, and create realistic but entirely fabricated videos. Deepfake technology, for instance, can produce hyper-realistic videos of public figures saying or doing things they never did. This has serious implications for political stability, public trust, and security. During elections, AI-generated fake news and propaganda can be used to mislead voters, manipulate opinions, and even incite violence. The rapid spread of misinformation through AI-driven algorithms on social media platforms has already contributed to political polarization and societal unrest. If left unchecked, AI's role in misinformation could undermine democracy and truth itself.

Job displacement and economic inequality are also growing concerns as AI automation advances. Many industries are replacing human workers with AI-driven systems, leading to widespread job losses in manufacturing, customer service, transportation, and even white-collar professions. While AI creates new job opportunities, these often require specialized skills that many displaced workers do not possess. Without proper retraining and economic policies, AI-driven automation could deepen social and economic inequalities, leaving millions unemployed and struggling to adapt to a rapidly changing workforce.

Perhaps the most unsettling risk of AI is its potential misuse in security and warfare. Governments and military organizations are increasingly investing in autonomous weapons and AI-driven surveillance systems. These technologies, if misused, could lead to a future where warfare is dictated by algorithms rather than human judgment. The prospect of AI-controlled drones, robotic soldiers, or cyber weapons that operate without human intervention raises ethical and existential questions about the role of AI in conflict. If AI systems make life-or-death decisions on their own, who is accountable for their actions?

Even in non-military applications, AI security risks are becoming more evident. AI-driven cyberattacks are on the rise, where hackers use machine learning algorithms to identify vulnerabilities in systems, evade detection, and execute sophisticated attacks. The same AI tools that strengthen cybersecurity are also being weaponized by cybercriminals, creating an ongoing arms race between security experts and malicious actors. AI's ability to learn and adapt means that future cyberattacks could become nearly impossible to predict or prevent.

Despite these warning signs, AI development continues at an accelerated pace, often outpacing regulatory efforts. While AI has the potential to bring immense benefits, failing to address these risks could lead to widespread harm. Governments, researchers, and industry leaders must work together to establish strict ethical guidelines, improve AI transparency, and develop mechanisms for accountability. The first warning signs of AI's dangers are already here—it is up to humanity to heed them before they escalate into irreversible consequences.

Chapter 2
The Benefits of AI—A New Age of Possibilities

Artificial Intelligence (AI) is ushering in a new age of possibilities, transforming nearly every industry and aspect of human life. From revolutionizing healthcare and education to optimizing businesses and advancing scientific research, AI's potential for positive impact is immense. Unlike traditional computing, which follows explicit instructions, AI has the ability to learn, adapt, and make decisions based on vast amounts of data. This fundamental shift has enabled breakthroughs that were once thought to be impossible, paving the way for a smarter, more efficient, and interconnected world.

One of AI's most significant benefits is its ability to **enhance human capabilities** rather than simply replace them. AI-powered tools are augmenting human intelligence, allowing professionals to work more efficiently and make better-informed decisions. In medicine, AI assists doctors by analyzing medical images, detecting diseases at early stages, and recommending personalized treatment plans based on patient data. In education, AI-driven tutoring systems provide customized learning experiences tailored to individual students, helping bridge gaps in knowledge and making education more accessible. Across various industries, AI is not just automating tasks but also serving as a powerful collaborator, enabling humans to achieve more than ever before.

Another major advantage of AI is its ability to **process and analyze vast amounts of data at speeds far beyond human capability**. Businesses are leveraging AI-powered analytics to optimize supply chains, predict customer behavior, and improve operational efficiency. Financial institutions use AI-driven models to detect fraudulent transactions, assess credit risk, and provide automated financial advice. In marketing, AI enables hyper-personalization, ensuring that customers receive content, product recommendations, and advertisements tailored to their specific preferences. This ability to extract meaningful insights from data is transforming decision-making, allowing organizations to become more agile and responsive to changing trends.

AI is also playing a crucial role in **solving some of the world's most pressing challenges**. In environmental science, AI models are being used to track climate change, optimize renewable energy sources, and develop sustainable solutions for reducing carbon emissions. Smart grids powered by AI help manage electricity distribution, reducing waste and improving energy efficiency. AI-driven agricultural technologies optimize irrigation, monitor crop health, and predict pest outbreaks, helping to increase food production while minimizing environmental impact. These applications highlight AI's potential not just to improve industries but also to contribute to the well-being of the planet.

Beyond practical applications, AI is **enhancing creativity and innovation** in ways that were once unimaginable. AI-generated art, music, and literature are pushing the boundaries of creative expression, allowing artists and writers to explore new forms of storytelling. In the entertainment industry, AI is revolutionizing content creation, from generating realistic visual effects to composing original soundtracks. Even in scientific research, AI is accelerating discoveries in fields such as drug development, quantum computing, and space exploration. AI's ability to simulate complex systems and process massive datasets is enabling researchers to make breakthroughs that could take decades using traditional methods.

Despite its remarkable benefits, AI's rapid advancement also raises important ethical considerations, including concerns about bias, privacy, and job displacement. However, these challenges can be addressed through responsible development, regulation, and collaboration between policymakers, businesses, and AI researchers. If harnessed correctly, AI has the potential to be one of the greatest tools humanity has ever created—one that enhances lives, drives innovation, and helps solve global problems.

As AI continues to evolve, the question is not whether we should embrace it, but how we can ensure that its benefits are distributed fairly and ethically. The new age of possibilities that AI presents is only just beginning, and the decisions we make today will shape the future of this transformative technology. By leveraging AI responsibly, humanity has the opportunity to create a future where technology works in harmony with human values, unlocking unprecedented progress for generations to come.

AI in Healthcare: Saving Lives and Improving Well-being

Artificial Intelligence (AI) is transforming the healthcare industry, revolutionizing the way diseases are diagnosed, treatments are administered, and patient care is managed. By leveraging vast amounts of medical data, machine learning algorithms, and predictive analytics, AI is enabling faster, more accurate diagnoses, reducing human errors, and making healthcare more accessible and efficient. From early disease detection and robotic-assisted surgeries to AI-powered drug development and personalized medicine, AI is reshaping the medical landscape, ultimately saving lives and improving overall well-being.

One of the most significant ways AI is contributing to healthcare is through **early disease detection and diagnosis**. AI-powered tools can analyze medical images, such as X-rays, MRIs, and CT scans, with remarkable accuracy, often surpassing human radiologists in detecting abnormalities. For instance, AI algorithms have been developed to identify early signs of cancer, allowing for earlier intervention and better patient outcomes. Deep learning models trained on vast datasets of retinal images can detect diabetic retinopathy, a leading cause of blindness, at a much earlier stage than traditional screening methods. Similarly, AI-driven diagnostic tools are being used to detect neurological conditions such as Alzheimer's and Parkinson's disease, helping doctors provide timely and effective treatments.

AI is also playing a crucial role in **personalized medicine**, tailoring treatments to individual patients based on their genetic makeup, medical history, and lifestyle. Traditional treatments often follow a one-size-fits-all approach, but AI-driven predictive models can analyze genetic data and suggest customized treatment plans that are more effective for each patient. This is particularly beneficial in oncology, where AI is being used to match cancer patients with the most suitable therapies based on their tumor's specific genetic mutations. AI-driven drug discovery is another breakthrough in personalized medicine, as machine learning models can predict how different compounds will interact with human cells, speeding up the drug development process and reducing the time it takes for new treatments to reach patients.

Another area where AI is making a significant impact is **robotic-assisted surgeries**. AI-powered robotic systems enhance the precision and accuracy of surgical procedures, reducing the risk of complications and improving patient recovery times. These robotic assistants can perform minimally invasive surgeries with greater precision than human hands, leading to less blood loss, smaller incisions, and quicker healing. AI-driven surgical robots are also capable of learning from past procedures, continuously improving their performance and assisting surgeons in making more informed decisions during operations.

AI is also transforming **patient care and hospital management**, making healthcare more efficient and accessible. AI-powered chatbots and virtual health assistants can provide patients with 24/7 medical support, answering their questions, scheduling appointments, and even offering preliminary diagnoses based on symptoms. This not only improves patient engagement but also reduces the burden on healthcare professionals, allowing them to focus on more critical cases. AI-driven hospital management systems optimize resource allocation, ensuring that hospital beds, medical equipment, and staff are utilized efficiently. Predictive analytics can help hospitals anticipate patient admission rates, enabling better planning for emergency situations and reducing wait times for critical care.

Furthermore, AI is playing a key role in **epidemic prediction and disease prevention**. AI models can analyze vast amounts of health data, including social media posts, travel patterns, and environmental factors, to predict disease outbreaks before they happen. During the COVID-19 pandemic, AI was used to track the spread of the virus, develop treatment protocols, and assist in vaccine research. By identifying potential health crises before they escalate, AI enables governments and healthcare organizations to implement preventive measures, ultimately saving lives on a global scale.

Despite its immense benefits, AI in healthcare also comes with challenges, including concerns about data privacy, algorithmic biases, and the need for regulatory oversight. Ensuring that AI systems are transparent, fair, and secure is crucial for maintaining public trust and preventing ethical dilemmas in medical decision-making. However, with responsible development and implementation, AI has the potential to revolutionize healthcare, making it more efficient, accurate, and patient-centered.

As AI continues to evolve, its role in healthcare will only expand, offering new ways to improve patient outcomes, streamline medical processes, and enhance overall well-being. From detecting diseases earlier to providing personalized treatments and assisting in surgeries, AI is not just changing medicine—it is saving lives and shaping the future of healthcare.

Automation and the Future of Work

Automation and the Future of Work

The rapid advancement of artificial intelligence (AI) and automation is transforming the global workforce, reshaping industries, and redefining the nature of work itself. As machines and algorithms take on tasks traditionally performed by humans, businesses are experiencing increased efficiency, reduced operational costs, and enhanced productivity. However, this shift also raises critical questions about job security, economic inequality, and the skills required for the future job market. The impact of automation on employment is complex, with both opportunities and challenges that will shape the workforce of tomorrow.

One of the most significant benefits of automation is its ability to handle repetitive and time-consuming tasks with greater speed and accuracy than human workers. Automated systems are already being used in industries such as manufacturing, logistics, and customer service to streamline processes and minimize human error. In factories, robotic arms perform assembly-line tasks with precision, increasing production rates while reducing workplace injuries. In the retail sector, self-checkout systems and AI-powered chatbots are replacing cashiers and customer service representatives, enabling businesses to operate more efficiently. Even in fields such as journalism and legal services, AI-driven software is being used to generate reports, draft contracts, and analyze large volumes of data, significantly reducing the time required for manual processing.

However, while automation enhances productivity, it also raises concerns about **job displacement**. Many roles that involve routine, repetitive tasks are at risk of being fully automated, leading to workforce reductions in certain sectors. Studies suggest that millions of jobs could be lost due to automation, particularly in industries that rely heavily on manual labor. For example, autonomous vehicles threaten to replace taxi and truck drivers, while AI-powered algorithms could eliminate administrative roles in finance and healthcare. The displacement of workers due to automation poses a significant challenge, as many employees may struggle to find new employment opportunities without acquiring new skills.

Despite fears of widespread job loss, automation also has the potential to create new opportunities and industries. Historically, technological advancements have led to job transformation rather than complete elimination. While some roles may become obsolete, new jobs will emerge that require human creativity, problem-solving, and emotional intelligence—skills that AI and machines cannot easily replicate. For instance, the rise of automation has led to increased demand for AI specialists, robotics engineers, and data scientists. Similarly, as businesses integrate more AI-driven solutions, there will be a growing need for professionals who can oversee, maintain, and regulate these systems.

The key to adapting to the future of work lies in **reskilling and upskilling the workforce.** Governments, educational institutions, and businesses must collaborate to provide training programs that equip workers with the skills needed for an AI-driven economy. This includes technical skills such as coding, data analysis, and cybersecurity, as well as soft skills like critical thinking, creativity, and adaptability. By investing in lifelong learning initiatives, societies can ensure that workers remain competitive and capable of transitioning into new roles as automation reshapes industries.

Another major consideration in the automation revolution is **economic inequality**. While businesses benefit from increased efficiency and lower labor costs, the financial gains are often concentrated among a small group of corporations and investors, potentially widening the wealth gap. Without proper policies and regulations, automation could lead to greater disparities in income distribution, leaving many workers struggling to adapt. Governments may need to consider measures such as universal basic income (UBI) or social safety nets to support displaced workers during this transition period.

Ultimately, the future of work will not be defined by automation alone but by how societies choose to adapt to these changes. While AI and robotics are undeniably reshaping the job market, human ingenuity, emotional intelligence, and adaptability remain irreplaceable. By embracing automation as a tool for innovation rather than a threat, businesses and workers alike can navigate the challenges of the evolving workforce and build a future where technology enhances human potential rather than diminishes it.

AI and Scientific Breakthroughs: Accelerating Discovery

Artificial Intelligence (AI) is revolutionizing scientific research, accelerating discoveries, and pushing the boundaries of human knowledge. Traditionally, scientific breakthroughs have required years of experimentation, data collection, and analysis. However, with AI's ability to process massive datasets, identify patterns, and make complex predictions, researchers can now achieve groundbreaking discoveries in a fraction of the time. From medical advancements and drug discovery to space exploration and climate research, AI is transforming the way we approach science, making previously unimaginable feats possible.

One of the most profound areas where AI is making a difference is medical research and drug discovery. Developing new drugs is a lengthy and expensive process, often taking over a decade and costing billions of dollars. AI-powered models can analyze vast amounts of biomedical data, predict how different chemical compounds will interact with human cells, and identify potential drug candidates with remarkable speed and accuracy. For example, AI has been used to identify promising treatments for diseases such as cancer, Alzheimer's, and even COVID-19. DeepMind's AlphaFold, an AI system capable of predicting protein structures, has solved one of biology's greatest challenges—determining the 3D shapes of proteins. This breakthrough is expected to accelerate drug development and improve our understanding of genetic diseases.

AI is also transforming genomics and personalized medicine, enabling researchers to analyze complex genetic data and tailor treatments to individual patients. AI algorithms can identify genetic mutations linked to diseases, helping doctors develop customized treatment plans based on a patient's unique genetic makeup. By leveraging machine learning, scientists can predict how a patient will respond to a particular drug, improving treatment effectiveness while minimizing side effects. AI-driven genomic research is paving the way for precision medicine, where treatments are no longer one-size-fits-all but are instead tailored to the specific needs of each individual.

Beyond healthcare, AI is playing a crucial role in space exploration and astrophysics. The vastness of the universe presents an overwhelming amount of data, making it nearly impossible for humans to analyze manually. AI-powered telescopes can scan the cosmos for exoplanets, detect gravitational waves, and identify patterns in astronomical data that were previously undetectable. NASA and other space agencies are using AI to analyze data from Mars rovers, optimize spacecraft navigation, and even search for signs of extraterrestrial life. AI-driven simulations allow astrophysicists to model the evolution of galaxies, black holes, and dark matter, leading to new insights into the nature of the universe.

In the fight against climate change, AI is being used to develop sustainable solutions, optimize energy use, and predict environmental changes. AI-powered climate models can analyze historical weather patterns, predict extreme weather events, and assess the impact of global warming with greater accuracy. Machine learning algorithms are also helping researchers develop innovative renewable energy solutions, such as optimizing solar panel efficiency and improving wind turbine placement. AI is even being used to monitor deforestation, track endangered species, and manage natural resources more effectively, contributing to a more sustainable planet.

AI is also transforming materials science, enabling researchers to discover new materials with extraordinary properties. Traditionally, finding new materials for industrial or medical applications required years of trial and error. AI-powered simulations can now predict how different materials will behave under specific conditions, drastically reducing the time needed for discovery. For example, researchers are using AI to develop superconductors, ultra-lightweight materials for aerospace, and even self-healing materials that could revolutionize manufacturing.

Despite these incredible advancements, AI's role in scientific research is not without challenges. The accuracy of AI models depends on the quality of data they are trained on, and biases in datasets can lead to flawed conclusions. Additionally, while AI can assist researchers in making predictions, human intuition, creativity, and ethical considerations remain essential in scientific discovery.

Nevertheless, AI is proving to be one of the most powerful tools in modern science. By automating data analysis, accelerating simulations, and uncovering hidden patterns, AI is enabling scientists to achieve breakthroughs at an unprecedented rate. As AI technology continues to evolve, it has the potential to unlock answers to some of humanity's greatest scientific mysteries, leading to new innovations that will shape the future of medicine, space exploration, sustainability, and beyond.

AI as a Creative Force: Music, Art, and Literature

Artificial Intelligence (AI) is no longer confined to the realms of logic, analytics, and automation—it is now actively participating in the world of human creativity. AI is revolutionizing artistic expression, pushing the boundaries of music composition, visual art, and literature in ways that were once unimaginable. While creativity has traditionally been considered an exclusively human trait, AI-powered tools are proving that machines can generate compelling and thought-provoking creative works. By learning from vast amounts of data and patterns, AI is not only assisting artists but also creating entirely new forms of artistic expression.

One of the most fascinating applications of AI in creativity is in music composition and production. AI-powered music generators, such as OpenAI's MuseNet and Google's Magenta, can compose entire pieces in different styles, from classical symphonies to modern pop songs. These systems analyze vast datasets of musical compositions, identifying patterns in melody, harmony, and rhythm to generate original pieces that sound remarkably human-made. AI is also being used in music production, helping artists experiment with new sounds, automate mixing and mastering processes, and even compose personalized soundtracks for video games and films. Some AI-generated compositions have been so sophisticated that they challenge the notion of human exclusivity in the realm of musical creativity.

In the field of visual art, AI-generated works have gained global recognition, even selling for thousands of dollars at art auctions. One of the most famous examples is Portrait of Edmond de Belamy, an AI-generated painting that sold for $432,500 at a Christie's auction in 2018. AI tools like DeepArt, Runway ML, and DALL·E can create stunning images by analyzing thousands of artworks, learning artistic styles, and then generating unique pieces based on user inputs. AI is also being used in digital painting and animation, assisting artists in refining their work or generating entirely new concepts. AI-generated art blurs the line between human and machine creativity, raising philosophical questions about authorship, originality, and artistic value.

In literature and storytelling, AI is becoming an increasingly powerful tool for writers. Language models such as GPT-4 can generate entire articles, stories, and even poetry, mimicking different writing styles with remarkable accuracy. AI-powered tools assist authors by generating ideas, suggesting plot developments, and even completing unfinished manuscripts. Some AI-generated books have been published, sparking debate about whether machines can truly replace human storytelling. While AI can produce grammatically correct and contextually relevant text, it lacks the emotional depth and lived experiences that define great literature. However, many writers are using AI as a collaborative tool, allowing machines to inspire new narratives while preserving human creativity.

The rise of AI-generated creativity has sparked ethical and philosophical debates about the role of machines in the arts. Can AI truly be creative, or is it merely replicating existing patterns? Should AI-generated works be credited to machines, programmers, or users? While AI is undeniably a powerful tool for creative exploration, it still lacks the ability to experience emotions, personal struggles, and deep insights that often fuel human creativity. Rather than replacing artists, AI is best seen as an enabler—a tool that expands creative possibilities and enhances human artistic expression.

As AI continues to evolve, its impact on music, art, and literature will only grow. Whether generating stunning visuals, composing mesmerizing symphonies, or assisting in storytelling, AI is proving that creativity is not solely a human endeavor. Instead, it is a collaboration between human intuition and machine intelligence, leading to a new era of artistic expression where imagination knows no limits.

Chapter 3
The Dark Side—Risks, Bias, and Control

As artificial intelligence (AI) continues to advance at an unprecedented pace, its transformative potential is met with growing concerns about the risks it poses to society. While AI has the capability to revolutionize industries, improve efficiency, and enhance decision-making, it also comes with unintended consequences that could disrupt economies, threaten personal freedoms, and even deepen existing societal inequalities. The darker side of AI is not just a distant dystopian scenario—it is already unfolding in various aspects of our daily lives, from biased decision-making systems and mass surveillance to the increasing concentration of power in the hands of a few corporations and governments. If left unchecked, AI's risks could outweigh its benefits, leading to a future where technology no longer serves humanity but instead dictates it.

One of the most pressing concerns surrounding AI is algorithmic bias, which arises when AI systems inadvertently reinforce discrimination and inequality. AI models are trained on historical data, and if this data contains biases—whether racial, gender-based, or socio-economic—AI systems can replicate and even amplify these biases. This has already been observed in hiring algorithms that favor certain demographic groups, facial recognition systems that misidentify people of color at disproportionately high rates, and predictive policing tools that unfairly target marginalized communities. Because AI is often perceived as an objective and neutral technology, biased decisions can go unchallenged, perpetuating systemic discrimination on an unprecedented scale.

Beyond bias, the issue of control and accountability looms large in discussions about AI's risks. As AI systems become more sophisticated, they are increasingly making decisions that impact people's lives—decisions about who gets a loan, which candidates are considered for a job, or even who gets flagged as a security threat. The problem is that many AI models operate as "black boxes," meaning their decision-making processes are not fully understood even by their own creators. This lack of transparency makes it difficult to challenge AI-driven decisions or hold anyone accountable when things go wrong. If AI systems are allowed to make high-stakes decisions without human oversight, society could face a future where individuals have little recourse against unfair or harmful outcomes.

Another alarming aspect of AI's darker side is its role in surveillance and social control. Governments and corporations are increasingly using AI-powered tools to monitor, predict, and influence human behavior. Facial recognition technology is being deployed in public spaces, social media algorithms are tracking personal preferences, and AI-driven data analytics are being used to manipulate political opinions. In authoritarian regimes, AI is already being used to suppress dissent and enforce ideological conformity through mass surveillance systems. Even in democratic societies, the unchecked use of AI for surveillance threatens personal privacy and civil liberties. If AI's ability to track and analyze human behavior continues to grow without regulation, individuals may find themselves living in a society where personal freedoms are significantly eroded.

Perhaps the most existential concern of all is the concentration of AI power in the hands of a few entities. The development and deployment of advanced AI systems are dominated by a handful of powerful corporations and governments that control vast amounts of data and computational resources. This raises concerns about monopolization, where a small elite determines how AI is used, who benefits from it, and how society is shaped by its influence. If AI is developed primarily for profit or political control rather than the common good, it could deepen economic disparities and create a future where a select few wield unprecedented power over the rest of humanity.

While AI has the potential to be a force for good, these risks highlight the urgent need for ethical frameworks, regulations, and global discussions on responsible AI development. Without proactive measures, AI could become a tool for discrimination, surveillance, and control rather than a means of empowerment. The challenge lies in ensuring that AI remains aligned with human values and does not become a system that prioritizes efficiency and profitability over fairness and justice. The dark side of AI is not inevitable, but it requires immediate and collective action to prevent its most harmful consequences from taking root in society.

Algorithmic Bias: The Silent Discrimination Machine

Artificial Intelligence (AI) is often portrayed as a neutral and objective technology, capable of making rational, data-driven decisions free from human prejudices. However, reality tells a different story. AI systems, particularly those based on machine learning, are only as unbiased as the data they are trained on. If the data reflects historical inequalities, social biases, or systemic discrimination, the AI will inherit and amplify these issues. This phenomenon, known as algorithmic bias, has become one of the most pressing ethical concerns in AI development. While AI has the potential to enhance decision-making, it can also reinforce discrimination, affecting critical areas such as hiring, policing, lending, healthcare, and more. The silent nature of algorithmic bias makes it even more dangerous—people often trust AI-driven decisions without realizing that they may be unfair or discriminatory.

One of the most alarming examples of algorithmic bias has been found in hiring and recruitment systems. Many companies use AI-powered tools to filter job applicants, analyze resumes, and even conduct automated interviews. However, studies have shown that these systems can be biased against certain demographic groups. For instance, Amazon once developed an AI-driven hiring tool that ended up discriminating against female applicants because it was trained on historical hiring data that favored male candidates. Since the AI learned from past patterns, it automatically downgraded resumes containing words like "women's" (as in "women's soccer team" or "women's leadership program"), reinforcing gender discrimination. Even after attempts to fix the system, biases remained, highlighting the difficulty of correcting discriminatory patterns once they are embedded in AI.

Another domain deeply affected by algorithmic bias is law enforcement and criminal justice. Predictive policing algorithms are used to analyze crime data and predict where crimes are likely to occur. However, these systems have disproportionately targeted communities of color because they are trained on historical crime data that reflects decades of racial profiling and over-policing in marginalized areas. For example, studies have shown that facial recognition software used by law enforcement has higher error rates when identifying Black and Asian individuals compared to white individuals. This has led to wrongful arrests and further mistrust between law enforcement and minority communities. When AI reinforces racial biases, it can perpetuate systemic injustice rather than eliminate it.

Algorithmic bias is also prevalent in financial services, where AI-driven credit scoring and loan approval systems determine who qualifies for loans and mortgages. Research has found that these systems can unintentionally discriminate against minority groups, denying them loans at higher rates than white applicants with similar financial backgrounds. Since AI models are trained on past financial data, they may replicate and reinforce patterns of economic inequality. This exacerbates the wealth gap, making it even harder for marginalized communities to access financial opportunities.

In healthcare, algorithmic bias has serious implications for patient outcomes. AI-powered diagnostic tools and treatment recommendation systems are increasingly being used to assist doctors, but studies have found that some of these tools perform less accurately for non-white patients. One prominent case involved an AI system designed to allocate healthcare resources, which systematically prioritized white patients over Black patients, even when their medical conditions were similar. This happened because the AI was trained on historical healthcare spending data, which reflected existing disparities in medical treatment. As a result, the AI learned to associate healthcare spending with medical need, without accounting for racial inequities in healthcare access.

Despite these concerning examples, algorithmic bias is not an inevitable flaw—it is a problem that can be mitigated through responsible AI development. Researchers and policymakers are now advocating for greater transparency, fairness, and accountability in

AI systems. This includes improving the diversity of training data, auditing AI models for bias, and ensuring that AI decision-making is interpretable and explainable. Companies and organizations deploying AI should prioritize ethical AI development by conducting bias impact assessments and implementing fairness constraints in their models.

Public awareness and regulatory action are also crucial in addressing algorithmic bias. Governments and institutions must enforce laws that prevent discriminatory AI practices and ensure that AI-driven decisions are subject to human oversight. Without proper regulation, AI risks becoming an invisible force that deepens inequality rather than eliminating it.

Algorithmic bias is a silent but powerful issue that affects millions of people worldwide. As AI continues to shape our lives, it is essential to recognize and address the biases embedded in these systems. AI should not be a tool that reinforces discrimination but one that promotes fairness, equity, and justice. The challenge now is ensuring that AI development aligns with these principles before biases become deeply entrenched in the systems that govern our world.

The Threat of Mass Surveillance and Privacy Erosion

In an era where artificial intelligence (AI) is deeply integrated into everyday life, concerns over mass surveillance and privacy erosion have become more pressing than ever. Governments, corporations, and intelligence agencies are deploying AI-powered surveillance systems at an unprecedented scale, tracking individuals' movements, online behaviors, and personal interactions. While proponents argue that these technologies enhance security, prevent crime, and streamline services, the darker reality is that mass surveillance poses a significant threat to individual freedoms, civil liberties, and democracy itself. Without proper regulations and safeguards, AI-driven surveillance can transform society into a digital panopticon—an environment where privacy is nonexistent, and citizens are constantly monitored without their consent.

One of the most pervasive tools of AI-powered surveillance is facial recognition technology. Governments around the world are increasingly using facial recognition systems to monitor public spaces, identify individuals in crowds, and track movements in real time. Countries such as China have already implemented vast surveillance networks, where AI-driven cameras monitor citizens on the streets, in shopping malls, and even in places of worship. These systems are often integrated with national databases, enabling authorities to identify and flag individuals within seconds. While facial recognition is promoted as a tool for crime prevention, it has also been used to suppress dissent, track political activists, and restrict freedom of expression. The fear of being constantly watched creates a chilling effect, discouraging people from engaging in protests, political discussions, or any activity that could be deemed undesirable by those in power.

AI-driven surveillance is not limited to physical spaces—it extends deep into the digital world, where every online action is tracked, analyzed, and stored. Social media platforms, search engines, and e-commerce websites collect vast amounts of user data, building detailed profiles based on browsing history, location data, and personal preferences. This data is then used for targeted advertising, behavior prediction, and even political manipulation. Governments and corporations can analyze online activities to determine individuals' beliefs, affiliations, and psychological tendencies, raising serious concerns about data privacy and personal autonomy. In some cases, AI algorithms can even predict future behaviors based on past interactions, allowing authorities or corporations to intervene before an action is taken.

The combination of AI and predictive analytics has led to the rise of pre-crime technologies, where law enforcement agencies use AI to predict criminal behavior before it happens. Predictive policing systems analyze crime data to identify "high-risk" individuals or areas, often leading to increased surveillance and law enforcement presence in specific communities. However, these systems are prone to bias, as they are trained on historical crime data that may reflect systemic discrimination. This means marginalized communities are disproportionately targeted, reinforcing racial profiling and deepening societal inequalities.

Beyond law enforcement, corporate surveillance has become an equally significant threat to privacy. Companies like Google, Facebook, and Amazon operate massive data collection ecosystems that track users across devices, applications, and even offline purchases. AI-powered analytics allow these corporations to anticipate consumer behavior, influence purchasing decisions, and manipulate user experiences. While some argue that this improves personalization and convenience, the trade-off is a loss of control over one's own digital footprint. Users are often unaware of the extent to which their data is being harvested and exploited, and in many cases, they have no meaningful way to opt out.

Perhaps the most alarming aspect of AI-driven mass surveillance is its potential for authoritarian control. When AI is used to monitor and influence citizens at scale, it can be weaponized by governments to suppress opposition, manipulate elections, and control narratives. Social credit systems, as seen in China, assign individuals scores based on their behavior, rewarding compliance and punishing dissent. In extreme cases, AI-driven surveillance could be used to identify and silence political opponents, journalists, and activists before they even take action. This level of control creates a society where fear replaces freedom, and individuals are forced to self-censor out of concern for potential repercussions.

The erosion of privacy through AI-driven surveillance is a global issue that demands urgent attention. While security and convenience are often cited as justifications for these technologies, they should not come at the expense of fundamental human rights. Governments must establish clear regulations to limit the scope of AI surveillance, ensuring that it is used responsibly and transparently. Individuals must also become more aware of how their data is collected and take steps to protect their digital privacy through encryption, secure browsing, and advocacy for stronger privacy laws.

Unchecked AI-driven mass surveillance is a direct threat to democracy, personal freedom, and human dignity. Without strong legal and ethical safeguards, society risks descending into an age where privacy is a relic of the past, and AI becomes a tool of control rather than empowerment. The fight to preserve privacy is not just about protecting personal data—it is about safeguarding the very essence of human autonomy in the digital age.

Deepfakes, Misinformation, and the AI War on Truth

Artificial Intelligence (AI) has become a powerful tool for creating, sharing, and manipulating information. While AI has enabled significant advancements in communication, content creation, and media, it has also given rise to an unprecedented challenge: the erosion of truth. Deepfake technology, AI-generated misinformation, and algorithm-driven content manipulation are reshaping public discourse, undermining trust in institutions, and fueling societal divisions. As AI-powered disinformation becomes more sophisticated, the line between fact and fiction is becoming increasingly blurred, creating what some experts call an "AI war on truth."

At the forefront of this crisis are deepfakes, AI-generated videos, images, and audio that can convincingly depict people saying or doing things they never actually did. Using deep learning models, AI can analyze vast amounts of existing footage and generate highly realistic but entirely fabricated content. Initially developed for entertainment and digital effects, deepfakes have quickly become a tool for deception, fraud, and political manipulation. Politicians, celebrities, and public figures have all been targeted by deepfake campaigns, raising concerns about how this technology can be used to spread false narratives. In 2018, a deepfake video of Barack Obama surfaced, where he appeared to say things he never actually said. While the video was created as an educational tool to highlight the dangers of deepfakes, it demonstrated the alarming ease with which AI can fabricate convincing falsehoods.

Beyond video manipulation, AI-driven misinformation has infiltrated social media and news platforms, distorting reality on a massive scale. AI-powered bots can generate and spread misleading news articles, conspiracy theories, and politically motivated propaganda with alarming efficiency. Social media algorithms prioritize engagement, often amplifying sensational or emotionally charged content, regardless of its accuracy. This has led to the viral spread of false information on topics ranging from health and science to politics and global affairs. The COVID-19 pandemic, for example, saw a surge in AI-generated misinformation, with misleading claims about treatments, vaccines, and government responses being shared millions of times online. The ability of AI to generate realistic but false content has made it increasingly difficult for the public to distinguish credible information from fabricated narratives.

The consequences of AI-driven misinformation are far-reaching. In the political sphere, deepfakes and AI-generated disinformation can be weaponized to influence elections, damage reputations, and manipulate public opinion. In 2020, concerns arose that AI-generated videos and misleading narratives could be used to interfere with democratic processes. Authoritarian governments have also taken advantage of AI-powered misinformation, using deepfakes and propaganda to suppress dissent, create confusion, and discredit opposition voices. The threat is not just that false information exists, but that it becomes nearly impossible for people to determine what is true, leading to a widespread erosion of trust in news, institutions, and even personal interactions.

In addition to politics, AI-generated misinformation has significant implications for cybersecurity and financial fraud. Scammers have begun using AI-generated voice deepfakes to impersonate executives and commit financial fraud. In one instance, a deepfake voice was used to trick a company into transferring $243,000, believing they were following the instructions of their CEO. AI is also being used to generate convincing phishing scams, making it easier for cybercriminals to deceive individuals and organizations.

The battle against AI-driven misinformation requires urgent action. Governments, tech companies, and researchers must work together to develop AI detection tools capable of identifying deepfakes and false content. Media literacy programs should be expanded to help the public recognize and critically evaluate digital content. Social media platforms must implement stricter policies to prevent the spread of AI-generated disinformation, ensuring that false narratives do not gain undue influence. AI itself can also be used as a weapon against misinformation, with machine learning models being trained to detect manipulated media and flag misleading content in real time.

However, addressing the AI war on truth is not just about technological solutions—it is about reinforcing trust in factual information, upholding ethical journalism, and maintaining transparency in content creation. If left unchecked, AI-driven misinformation has the potential to destabilize societies, undermine democratic institutions, and create a world where truth is entirely subjective. In this battle, preserving reality is not just a challenge—it is a necessity.

When AI Becomes a Weapon: Military and Cyber Threats

As artificial intelligence (AI) continues to evolve, its integration into military and cybersecurity operations is reshaping the landscape of warfare and global security. While AI has been a force for innovation and efficiency in many industries, its weaponization poses significant ethical, strategic, and existential risks. From autonomous weapons and AI-driven cyberattacks to automated surveillance and digital warfare, the increasing reliance on AI in military operations raises profound concerns about accountability, decision-making, and the potential for catastrophic consequences.

One of the most concerning developments in AI's militarization is the rise of autonomous weapons systems, often referred to as "killer robots." These systems are designed to identify, target, and eliminate threats without direct human intervention. Unlike traditional drones, which require human operators, AI-powered autonomous weapons can make real-time combat decisions, reacting faster than any human soldier. Countries such as the United States, China, and Russia are investing heavily in AI-driven military technology, including automated missile defense systems, robotic soldiers, and unmanned fighter jets. While these systems promise increased battlefield efficiency, they also raise critical ethical questions. Who is responsible if an AI-controlled weapon makes a fatal mistake? Can AI be trusted to distinguish between combatants and civilians in complex war zones? The potential for unintended escalations in conflicts is immense, as AI-driven warfare could remove the human hesitation that acts as a natural deterrent to military action.

Beyond physical warfare, AI is increasingly being used as a tool for cyber warfare and digital espionage. AI-powered hacking tools can analyze vast amounts of data, identify vulnerabilities, and execute cyberattacks with extreme precision. Unlike traditional cyber threats, AI-enhanced attacks can adapt and evolve in real time, making them far more difficult to detect and defend against. Governments and criminal organizations are using AI to conduct large-scale cyber espionage, targeting critical infrastructure, financial institutions, and even democratic processes. AI-driven disinformation campaigns, deepfake propaganda, and election interference have already demonstrated the ability of AI to manipulate public opinion and destabilize political systems.

One of the most significant cyber threats posed by AI is its ability to conduct automated, large-scale cyberattacks. AI-powered malware can autonomously search for weaknesses in computer networks, spreading faster than human hackers could ever achieve. This capability raises concerns about AI being weaponized for state-sponsored cyber warfare, where nations launch AI-driven attacks against adversaries' power grids, communication systems, and government databases. The potential for AI to be used in cyberterrorism is equally alarming—hacker groups could use AI to disable essential services, disrupt financial markets, or manipulate global supply chains.

AI's role in mass surveillance and intelligence gathering is another growing concern in global security. Governments are deploying AI-driven surveillance tools to track individuals, monitor communications, and analyze behavioral patterns. While these technologies are often justified as counterterrorism measures, they can also be used to suppress political dissent, silence opposition groups, and violate fundamental human rights. The use of AI in military surveillance, facial recognition, and predictive analytics allows states to preemptively identify and neutralize perceived threats—but at what cost to civil liberties and democratic freedoms?

Despite these threats, AI also plays a crucial role in defensive cybersecurity and threat detection. AI-powered security systems can analyze vast networks for anomalies, detect cyber threats before they materialize, and automate responses to prevent data breaches. Governments and corporations are investing in AI-driven cybersecurity frameworks to protect critical infrastructure from AI-powered attacks. However, the challenge lies in the ongoing arms race between AI-powered offense and AI-powered defense. As AI-driven cyber threats become more sophisticated, security measures must continually evolve to counteract them.

The weaponization of AI is no longer a concept of the distant future—it is already here. The challenge for policymakers, military leaders, and technology developers is to ensure that AI is used responsibly, with clear ethical and legal frameworks governing its deployment. International agreements on AI in warfare, similar to nuclear arms control treaties, may become necessary to prevent the unchecked use of AI-driven weapons. Without such measures, AI's role in military and cyber warfare could lead to a new era of conflicts that are faster, deadlier, and harder to control.

As AI continues to advance, humanity faces a pivotal question: Will AI be used to enhance global security, or will it become the catalyst for a new kind of warfare, where machines make life-and-death decisions with no human oversight? The answer will shape the future of both warfare and global stability.

Chapter 4
The Economic Disruption— Winners and Losers

The rapid advancement of artificial intelligence (AI) is causing profound economic shifts, fundamentally altering industries, job markets, and financial systems. While AI offers unprecedented efficiency, productivity, and economic growth, it also presents challenges that could widen income disparities, displace traditional jobs, and consolidate power within a few dominant players. As AI continues to reshape the global economy, societies must grapple with the question: Who benefits from this technological revolution, and who is left behind?

One of the most immediate and significant impacts of AI on the economy is job displacement and workforce transformation. Automation, powered by AI, is replacing human labor in various industries, particularly in repetitive and routine tasks. In manufacturing, robotic systems now perform assembly-line work with precision, speed, and reliability, reducing the need for human workers. In the retail and service industries, AI-driven chatbots, automated checkout systems, and virtual assistants are handling customer interactions that were once managed by employees. Even white-collar professions such as law, finance, and healthcare are experiencing automation, with AI-driven software handling legal document analysis, stock trading, and even medical diagnoses. While AI increases efficiency, it also raises concerns about mass unemployment, particularly for low-skilled workers whose jobs are more susceptible to automation.

However, AI is not just a force of job destruction—it is also a catalyst for job creation and new economic opportunities. While some traditional roles may disappear, AI is generating demand for new skills and professions. Fields such as AI development, data science, cybersecurity, and AI ethics are rapidly expanding, creating new career paths. Businesses and governments are investing in AI training programs to equip workers with the skills needed to thrive in an AI-driven economy. Additionally, AI-powered tools are enabling entrepreneurs and small businesses to compete in markets that were once dominated by large corporations. Automation reduces overhead costs, allowing startups to scale more efficiently and innovate in ways that were previously unattainable.

AI is also driving economic inequality, as the benefits of automation and AI adoption are not evenly distributed. Large technology companies with the resources to develop and deploy AI systems are gaining a disproportionate share of the economic rewards. Tech giants such as Google, Amazon, and Microsoft are leveraging AI to dominate industries, from cloud computing and e-commerce to digital advertising and AI-driven services. This consolidation of AI power creates monopolistic dynamics where a handful of corporations control vast amounts of data, resources, and wealth. As a result, smaller businesses and workers who cannot keep up with AI-driven efficiencies risk being marginalized, leading to a widening gap between the economic "winners" and "losers."

Another major concern is the impact of AI on global trade and economic power dynamics. Countries that lead in AI research and development are gaining a significant economic advantage, while nations that lag behind face economic stagnation. The AI race between the United States and China highlights the geopolitical significance of AI, as both countries invest heavily in AI infrastructure, research, and military applications. Developing nations, which rely on labor-intensive industries, may struggle to compete in a world where AI-driven automation reduces the demand for human labor. Without strategic investments in AI education and infrastructure, some economies risk falling behind in the AI-driven global order.

Despite these challenges, AI also presents opportunities for economic growth and improved quality of life. AI-driven automation in agriculture is increasing food production while reducing costs. AI-powered healthcare innovations are improving patient outcomes and reducing medical expenses. In financial services, AI is making lending and investment decisions more efficient, helping businesses access capital faster. If managed responsibly, AI has the potential to create a more productive, innovative, and prosperous global economy.

The key to navigating the economic disruption caused by AI lies in education, policy-making, and strategic adaptation. Governments must implement policies that ensure AI-driven prosperity is shared across society, rather than concentrated among a privileged few. This includes investing in AI education programs, supporting displaced workers through retraining initiatives, and implementing regulatory frameworks that prevent AI-driven monopolization. Businesses must adopt responsible AI practices, ensuring that AI augments human labor rather than replacing it entirely.

AI is not inherently good or bad—it is a tool that can either deepen economic inequality or drive inclusive growth. The future of

AI-driven economies depends on how societies choose to integrate this technology into their economic systems. Will AI be a force that empowers all, or will it be a tool that benefits only a select few? The answer will define the winners and losers of the AI revolution.

AI's Impact on Job Markets and Labor

The rise of artificial intelligence (AI) is profoundly reshaping the job market, transforming industries, and redefining the nature of work itself. As AI-driven automation continues to advance, concerns about job displacement, shifting labor demands, and economic inequality have become central to discussions about the future of work. While AI presents opportunities for increased efficiency, innovation, and new job creation, it also threatens traditional employment structures, forcing workers and businesses to adapt to an evolving landscape.

One of the most immediate and visible effects of AI is automation replacing repetitive and routine jobs. Industries that rely heavily on manual or structured tasks are particularly vulnerable to automation. Manufacturing, logistics, and retail sectors have already seen widespread adoption of AI-powered robots and software, replacing human workers in assembly lines, warehouses, and customer service roles. Automated checkout systems in grocery stores, self-driving trucks in logistics, and AI-driven chatbots in customer support are just a few examples of how AI is reducing the demand for human labor in these fields. Even in white-collar professions, AI is being used to automate data analysis, legal document processing, and financial modeling, reducing the need for human input in traditionally high-skilled roles.

Despite fears of widespread job loss, AI is also creating new job opportunities and transforming existing roles. While automation may replace certain tasks, it is also generating demand for skills related to AI development, data science, cybersecurity, and AI ethics. New professions such as AI trainers, machine learning engineers, and algorithm auditors are emerging as AI technologies become more integrated into businesses. Additionally, many jobs will evolve rather than disappear entirely, requiring workers to develop new skill sets. For instance, instead of replacing doctors, AI is being used as a tool to assist in medical diagnosis and research, allowing healthcare professionals to focus on patient care while AI handles data-driven tasks.

A significant challenge posed by AI in the job market is the growing skills gap and the need for workforce adaptation. As industries increasingly rely on AI-driven solutions, the demand for workers with technical skills in AI, programming, and data analytics is rising. However, many workers in traditional industries may not have the necessary expertise to transition into these roles. Without proper retraining and reskilling initiatives, large segments of the workforce risk being left behind. Governments, businesses, and educational institutions must collaborate to implement training programs that equip workers with the skills required for an AI-driven economy. Lifelong learning initiatives, online courses, and vocational training programs will play a crucial role in helping workers adapt to the changing job market.

Another pressing concern is the economic and social inequalities AI may exacerbate. AI-driven automation benefits corporations by reducing labor costs and increasing efficiency, but it also risks widening the gap between high-skilled and low-skilled workers. Those who possess AI-related expertise will likely enjoy greater job security and higher wages, while those in vulnerable positions may face job displacement and financial instability. Without appropriate policies and economic adjustments, the benefits of AI could be concentrated among a small elite, leaving many workers struggling to find stable employment.

One potential solution to mitigate AI's disruptive impact on labor markets is rethinking economic policies and labor protections. Policymakers must consider implementing strategies such as universal basic income (UBI), wage subsidies, and labor market regulations to ensure that workers are not disproportionately affected by automation. Encouraging companies to adopt a "human-AI collaboration" approach—where AI enhances human productivity rather than replacing workers—can help create a more balanced transition into the AI-driven job market.

Ultimately, AI's impact on job markets and labor will depend on how societies choose to integrate it into their economic systems. While AI has the potential to improve efficiency and drive innovation, the challenge lies in ensuring that workers are equipped to thrive in an evolving job market. By prioritizing education, retraining, and inclusive policies, societies can harness AI's potential while safeguarding economic stability and job security for future generations.

The Rise of Automation: Who Will Be Left Behind?

The rapid advancement of artificial intelligence (AI) and automation is reshaping industries, revolutionizing economies, and redefining the way work is done. While automation brings undeniable benefits such as increased efficiency, cost savings, and productivity, it also presents a looming challenge—millions of workers risk being left behind. As machines take over repetitive, predictable tasks across various sectors, a growing divide is emerging between those who can adapt to this transformation and those who cannot. The question remains: who will thrive in an AI-driven economy, and who will struggle to keep up?

The first and most vulnerable group affected by automation is low-skill and repetitive-task workers. Jobs in manufacturing, retail, logistics, and customer service are among the most at risk. AI-powered robots are now performing assembly-line work in factories, automating quality control, and even handling warehouse operations without human intervention. Similarly, in the retail sector, self-checkout kiosks and automated inventory management systems are reducing the need for cashiers and stock clerks. In customer service, AI-driven chatbots and virtual assistants are handling inquiries, replacing human representatives in many businesses. These changes mean that workers in routine-based roles may find themselves displaced, often without the skills necessary to transition into new jobs.

Another group facing significant challenges is mid-level professionals in data-heavy fields. While automation has traditionally threatened blue-collar jobs, AI is increasingly capable of performing white-collar tasks that involve data processing, analysis, and repetitive decision-making. Financial analysts, legal assistants, accountants, and administrative personnel are seeing their roles increasingly automated through AI-driven systems. For instance, AI-powered legal software can now review contracts and conduct legal research far more efficiently than human paralegals. Similarly, AI-driven algorithms are being used in financial services to detect fraud, assess risk, and even manage investment portfolios, reducing the need for traditional financial analysts. This means that even knowledge-based workers who once felt secure in their professions are now at risk of being replaced by AI.

However, not everyone will be negatively affected by automation. High-skill workers in AI-driven fields, creative professions, and human-centered roles are likely to benefit from this technological shift. Jobs that require complex problem-solving, emotional intelligence, and human interaction—such as software development, healthcare, education, and psychology—will remain in demand. AI cannot replicate human creativity, empathy, or deep critical thinking, which means roles that emphasize these skills are safer from automation. Additionally, industries that develop and maintain AI systems—such as data science, cybersecurity, and AI ethics—will see a surge in demand for skilled professionals.

One of the biggest concerns regarding automation is the growing economic divide. Those who have access to education, retraining programs, and technological resources will have the opportunity to transition into AI-driven roles. Meanwhile, those without access to these opportunities—particularly workers in developing countries, older employees, and individuals from marginalized communities—may struggle to keep up. Without proper intervention, automation could widen the gap between the wealthy and the working class, concentrating economic power in the hands of corporations and tech-savvy professionals.

To prevent mass displacement, governments, businesses, and educational institutions must invest in workforce reskilling and adaptation programs. Lifelong learning initiatives, vocational training, and AI literacy programs will be crucial in preparing workers for the new economy. Governments may need to consider policies such as universal basic income (UBI), wage subsidies, and AI regulation to ensure that automation benefits society as a whole rather than deepening inequality.

The rise of automation is inevitable, but who gets left behind will depend on how societies choose to navigate this transition. With the right investments in education, skills training, and policy reforms, automation can be a tool for empowerment rather than exclusion. The challenge ahead is ensuring that AI's economic benefits are distributed equitably, creating a future where technology enhances human potential rather than rendering it obsolete.

Universal Basic Income and AI-Driven Inequality

The rise of artificial intelligence (AI) and automation is fundamentally reshaping the global economy, raising concerns about job displacement, wage stagnation, and widening economic inequality. As AI continues to automate tasks across industries, millions of workers risk losing their jobs, particularly those in roles that involve repetitive, manual, or administrative work. While AI is also creating new opportunities in emerging fields, many workers may struggle to transition due to skill mismatches and economic barriers. This growing divide between those who benefit from AI-driven prosperity and those left behind has intensified discussions around Universal Basic Income (UBI) as a potential solution to mitigate AI-driven inequality.

UBI is a policy proposal in which all citizens receive a fixed, unconditional sum of money from the government, regardless of employment status or income level. The idea is to provide financial security in an economy where traditional jobs are increasingly being replaced by automation. Proponents argue that UBI could act as a safety net, allowing individuals to maintain a basic standard of living even if they lose their jobs due to AI-driven automation. By providing people with a stable source of income, UBI could help prevent poverty, reduce economic anxiety, and empower individuals to pursue education, entrepreneurship, or creative endeavors without the immediate pressure of financial survival.

One of the main arguments for UBI is that AI-driven automation will disproportionately affect low-skill and middle-class workers, exacerbating economic inequality. In industries such as manufacturing, retail, transportation, and customer service, AI-powered systems and robots are already replacing human labor at an accelerating rate. While new jobs are being created in AI-related fields, these roles typically require advanced technical skills that many displaced workers do not have. Without adequate retraining and reskilling programs, a significant portion of the workforce may find itself permanently unemployed or underemployed. UBI could help bridge this gap by providing financial stability as workers transition to new careers in an AI-dominated job market.

However, UBI also has its challenges and criticisms. One of the primary concerns is the cost of implementation. Providing every citizen with a basic income would require significant government spending, raising questions about funding sources. Some proposals suggest taxing AI-driven corporations that benefit the most from automation, while others advocate for reallocating existing welfare programs into a streamlined UBI system. Critics also worry that UBI could discourage work, reduce productivity, and create inflationary pressures, though studies on pilot programs have yielded mixed results.

Another challenge is ensuring that UBI does not become a substitute for other social support systems. Some opponents argue that governments should focus on job creation, education, and retraining programs instead of distributing free money. Others believe that UBI should be implemented alongside policies that regulate AI deployment, prevent job monopolization by tech giants, and ensure fair wages for workers in AI-augmented roles.

Despite these challenges, several UBI experiments have provided valuable insights into its potential impact. In Finland, a pilot program found that recipients of basic income experienced reduced stress, improved well-being, and greater motivation to find work. Similar trials in Canada, Kenya, and the United States have shown that UBI can enhance financial security without significantly reducing workforce participation. These studies suggest that, when implemented correctly, UBI can serve as a stabilizing force in an AI-driven economy.

The debate over UBI is ultimately a debate about the future of work and economic justice. As AI continues to transform industries, societies must decide whether to allow wealth and power to concentrate among a small elite or to distribute AI-driven prosperity more equitably. UBI, if properly designed and funded, could help create a more inclusive economy where individuals have the freedom to pursue meaningful work, education, and personal growth without the constant fear of financial ruin. Whether or not UBI becomes a reality, one thing is clear: the rise of AI is forcing societies to rethink traditional economic models and explore new ways to ensure that technological progress benefits everyone, not just a privileged few.

The Role of Governments in Shaping AI Economics

As artificial intelligence (AI) continues to reshape industries, economies, and labor markets, governments play a crucial role in ensuring that its benefits are widely distributed and its risks are properly managed. AI has the potential to drive economic growth, increase productivity, and create new job opportunities, but it also poses significant challenges such as job displacement, widening income inequality, and the concentration of wealth and power in the hands of a few corporations. Without proper policies and regulations, AI could exacerbate existing economic divides and disrupt social stability. Governments must take proactive steps to shape AI economics in a way that fosters innovation, protects workers, and promotes equitable growth.

One of the primary responsibilities of governments is to develop and implement AI regulations that ensure fair competition and prevent monopolization. Currently, a handful of tech giants—such as Google, Amazon, Microsoft, and Tencent—dominate AI research and development, giving them unprecedented economic power. These corporations control vast amounts of data, computing resources, and AI talent, making it difficult for smaller businesses and startups to compete. Without regulatory oversight, this concentration of power could lead to a form of AI-driven economic inequality, where only a few companies benefit from automation while others struggle to survive. Governments must enforce antitrust laws, encourage fair competition, and support smaller AI startups to prevent monopolization and foster a more diverse and competitive AI ecosystem.

Another key role of governments is to invest in AI education, workforce reskilling, and training programs. As AI-driven automation disrupts traditional industries, millions of workers are at risk of job displacement. Governments must take the lead in funding and implementing large-scale retraining programs to help workers transition into AI-related fields. Initiatives such as free coding boot camps, AI literacy programs, and vocational training in emerging industries can equip workers with the skills needed to thrive in an AI-driven economy. Without proper investment in human capital, AI could lead to mass unemployment and exacerbate social inequalities.

In addition to workforce training, governments must redesign social safety nets to protect workers affected by AI-driven economic shifts. Universal Basic Income (UBI), wage subsidies, and tax reforms are among the policy options being considered to mitigate the negative effects of automation. If AI continues to replace human labor at a rapid pace, traditional employment models may no longer be sufficient to support large segments of the population. Governments must explore new economic frameworks that balance technological progress with social well-being, ensuring that automation benefits everyone rather than just a privileged few.

Furthermore, governments have a responsibility to regulate AI's impact on job quality and workers' rights. Many gig economy platforms, such as Uber and Amazon, use AI-driven algorithms to manage workers, determine wages, and assign tasks. While these platforms offer flexibility, they also create job insecurity, unpredictable wages, and exploitative conditions. Governments must establish clear labor protections for workers in AI-driven industries, ensuring fair wages, job stability, and ethical AI usage in employment decisions.

Another crucial area where governments must intervene is taxation and wealth redistribution in an AI-driven economy. As automation reduces the need for human labor, governments must reconsider traditional tax structures that rely heavily on income taxes. Some experts have proposed an AI or robot tax, where companies that replace human workers with AI-driven automation pay additional taxes to fund social programs and workforce training. Others advocate for taxing digital giants more effectively, ensuring that they contribute fairly to public infrastructure, education, and social welfare.

Beyond economic policies, governments must also promote ethical AI development and adoption. AI poses risks beyond job displacement, including bias in hiring, mass surveillance, and misinformation. Governments should work closely with AI researchers, private companies, and civil society to establish ethical guidelines for AI usage. This includes enforcing transparency in AI decision-making, preventing discrimination, and ensuring that AI-driven economic decisions align with human values.

Finally, governments must play a leading role in international cooperation and AI governance. AI is not just a national issue—it is a global force that transcends borders. Countries must collaborate on AI research, share best practices, and establish international agreements on AI ethics, cybersecurity, and fair economic policies. Without global cooperation, AI could fuel economic tensions, digital divide issues, and international conflicts.

In conclusion, governments have a vital role in shaping AI economics by fostering innovation, protecting workers, ensuring fair competition, and developing policies that promote equitable growth. AI's impact on the economy will depend on how effectively governments navigate this transition, balancing technological progress with social responsibility. By taking proactive measures, governments can ensure that AI serves as a tool for inclusive prosperity rather than a force that deepens economic divides. The choices made today will determine whether AI leads to a future of opportunity or a future of inequality.

Chapter 5
Can AI Be Aligned with Human Values?

As artificial intelligence (AI) becomes increasingly integrated into society, a critical question emerges: Can AI be aligned with human values? AI now influences everything from decision-making in healthcare and criminal justice to financial markets and military applications. Its impact is profound, yet its ability to act in ways that reflect ethical and moral human values remains uncertain. While AI has the potential to enhance human well-being, improve efficiency, and drive innovation, it also poses ethical dilemmas that challenge our fundamental principles of fairness, accountability, and justice. The alignment problem—ensuring that AI systems act in accordance with human values and societal norms—has become one of the most pressing issues in AI research and policy.

The challenge of aligning AI with human values begins with defining what those values are. Human morality is complex, diverse, and often subjective, varying across cultures, religions, and ideologies. What one group considers ethical may be viewed differently by another. AI systems, on the other hand, operate based on mathematical models and data-driven decision-making, which lack intrinsic moral reasoning. As a result, the values embedded in AI are often determined by the developers who create them, raising concerns about bias, representation, and unintended consequences.

One of the key risks of AI misalignment is algorithmic bias, where AI systems make decisions that reinforce existing inequalities and discrimination. AI models are trained on historical data, and if that data contains biases—whether related to race, gender, or socio-economic status—the AI system can perpetuate and even amplify these biases. This has been observed in hiring algorithms that favor male applicants, predictive policing systems that disproportionately target minority communities, and facial recognition technology that misidentifies individuals based on race. If AI systems are to align with human values, they must be designed to recognize and mitigate these biases rather than reinforce them.

Another critical issue is AI decision-making and accountability. AI operates autonomously in many areas, including self-driving cars, financial trading, and medical diagnostics. When AI makes a mistake, who is responsible? Should the blame fall on the developers, the companies deploying the AI, or the AI system itself? This lack of accountability creates ethical and legal dilemmas, particularly in high-stakes applications where AI decisions can mean life or death. Ensuring AI alignment with human values requires establishing clear frameworks for responsibility and transparency in AI decision-making.

Furthermore, AI must be aligned not just with ethical considerations but also with human dignity, privacy, and autonomy. AI-powered surveillance, data tracking, and personalized content algorithms have raised concerns about mass manipulation and loss of personal freedoms. Governments and corporations increasingly use AI to monitor behavior, predict actions, and influence decision-making. Without ethical guidelines, AI could erode fundamental rights rather than enhance them. Ethical AI must prioritize human autonomy, ensuring that people retain control over decisions that affect their lives.

The question of AI alignment is not just a technical challenge—it is also a philosophical and political one. Researchers, policymakers, and technologists must work together to create AI systems that uphold democratic values, protect human rights, and foster fairness. The alignment of AI with human values requires a multidisciplinary approach that combines ethics, law, psychology, and technology to ensure that AI serves humanity rather than undermines it.

Ultimately, the future of AI alignment depends on the choices made today. Will AI be designed to reflect the best of humanity, or will it evolve in ways that diverge from our moral and ethical frameworks? By proactively addressing these challenges, we can ensure that AI remains a tool that supports human progress rather than a force that compromises it. The journey toward AI alignment is complex, but it is a necessary one if we are to harness the full potential of AI while safeguarding our collective values.

The Challenge of Defining Ethical AI

As artificial intelligence (AI) becomes increasingly integrated into society, the question of ethics has taken center stage. AI now plays a role in decision-making processes across industries, from healthcare and finance to law enforcement and social media. However, defining what constitutes ethical AI remains a complex and unresolved challenge. Unlike traditional technologies, AI operates autonomously, learning from vast amounts of data to make predictions and decisions—often without human oversight. This raises critical questions: What values should AI systems uphold? Who decides what is ethical? And how can we ensure AI aligns with the diverse moral perspectives of global societies?

One of the primary difficulties in defining ethical AI is the subjectivity of ethics itself. Human morality is not universal; it is shaped by culture, religion, history, and personal beliefs. What one society considers ethical may be viewed differently in another. For example, AI-powered facial recognition used for security purposes might be acceptable in one country but seen as an invasion of privacy in another. Similarly, an AI-driven hiring tool that prioritizes efficiency may unintentionally overlook the importance of diversity and inclusion. Since AI operates on predefined rules and data, determining whose ethical framework should guide AI decision-making is a challenge that requires global cooperation and dialogue.

Another major obstacle is bias in AI systems, which can lead to discriminatory and unfair outcomes. AI learns from historical data, and if that data reflects past inequalities, the AI will likely replicate and reinforce them. Biased hiring algorithms, racial profiling in predictive policing, and unfair lending practices in finance are just a few examples of AI systems reflecting the prejudices present in the data they were trained on. Despite efforts to mitigate bias, AI remains vulnerable to the ethical shortcomings embedded in society. Ethical AI requires not only better data collection and filtering but also active oversight to ensure fairness and equity.

The issue of accountability and transparency further complicates ethical AI. When AI makes decisions that affect people's lives—such as approving loans, diagnosing medical conditions, or recommending prison sentences—who is responsible for mistakes? In traditional decision-making processes, humans can be held accountable, but AI lacks personal responsibility. Companies that deploy AI may argue that errors are a result of the algorithm rather than intentional bias. This "black box" problem—where AI operates in ways even its developers do not fully understand—makes it difficult to assign accountability and correct unethical outcomes. Ethical AI must prioritize transparency, ensuring that AI models are explainable and that decision-making processes can be audited.

Another ethical dilemma is privacy and surveillance. AI-driven technologies, such as facial recognition, data tracking, and personalized algorithms, have raised concerns about mass surveillance and manipulation. Governments and corporations collect vast amounts of personal data to optimize AI models, often without users' informed consent. Ethical AI must strike a balance between data-driven innovation and the protection of individual privacy. This includes creating robust regulations that prevent AI from being used to exploit personal information for profit or social control.

AI also raises concerns about autonomy and human agency. As AI systems become more capable of making independent decisions, the risk of humans losing control over AI-driven processes increases. Autonomous weapons, AI-driven financial trading, and automated content moderation on social media demonstrate the extent to which AI can operate with minimal human intervention. Ethical AI must ensure that humans retain decision-making power over critical areas where AI decisions could have serious ethical implications.

Despite these challenges, progress is being made toward defining ethical AI. Governments, research institutions, and tech companies are developing frameworks and guidelines to promote fairness, transparency, and accountability in AI development. Organizations like the European Union, the United Nations, and AI ethics research groups are working to create international standards for responsible AI use. However, enforcement remains a challenge, as ethical AI regulations often lag behind rapid technological advancements.

In conclusion, defining ethical AI is a complex, multidimensional challenge that requires collaboration between governments, businesses, researchers, and society at large. While AI has the potential to enhance human well-being, it also poses risks that must be carefully managed. Ethical AI must prioritize fairness, transparency, privacy, and human oversight to ensure that AI serves as a tool for progress rather than a source of harm. The challenge is not just about making AI ethical—it is about ensuring that ethics evolve alongside AI to meet the needs of a rapidly changing world.

Human Morality vs. Machine Decision-Making

As artificial intelligence (AI) continues to evolve, it increasingly takes on decision-making roles that were once the exclusive domain of humans. AI systems now make choices in areas such as hiring, healthcare, criminal justice, and financial lending—decisions that can have profound and lasting consequences for individuals and society. However, AI lacks the moral reasoning, intuition, and empathy that humans rely on when making ethical judgments. This raises an essential question: Can machine decision-making ever align with human morality? The growing divide between human ethics and AI-driven choices presents one of the most complex challenges in the development of responsible AI.

One of the fundamental differences between human morality and machine decision-making is that human ethics are deeply influenced by culture, experience, and emotions, while AI operates solely on logic and data patterns. Morality is not a fixed set of rules; it evolves over time and differs across societies, religions, and individual beliefs. Humans take into account contextual factors, intent, and the emotional impact of their decisions. AI, on the other hand, follows algorithms that optimize for efficiency, accuracy, and predetermined objectives. This difference becomes particularly problematic when AI is tasked with making decisions in morally sensitive areas.

For example, consider AI in criminal justice. Predictive policing algorithms analyze historical crime data to determine where crimes are likely to occur and who might be at risk of committing an offense. However, these systems often reinforce racial and socioeconomic biases present in the data, leading to discriminatory policing practices. A human judge may take into account personal circumstances, rehabilitation potential, and social conditions when making sentencing decisions, whereas an AI-driven system simply calculates risk scores based on statistical probabilities. The result is a rigid, dehumanized approach to justice that can perpetuate existing inequalities rather than addressing them.

Another major ethical dilemma arises in healthcare AI. AI is now being used to diagnose diseases, recommend treatments, and even decide which patients receive life-saving care in resource-limited situations. In a medical triage scenario, a human doctor may consider factors beyond survival probability, such as a patient's personal responsibilities, family situation, or quality of life after treatment. AI, however, is programmed to prioritize efficiency, often making decisions based on cold statistical analysis. If left unchecked, machine decision-making in healthcare could lead to ethical violations where human dignity is disregarded in favor of pure optimization.

One of the most well-known debates surrounding machine ethics is the autonomous vehicle dilemma, often referred to as the "trolley problem" of AI. If a self-driving car is faced with an unavoidable accident, should it prioritize the safety of its passengers, pedestrians, or the least number of casualties? A human driver might make a split-second moral judgment based on instinct and emotion, while an AI system must rely on pre-programmed decision trees. The ethical implications of who gets to "write the rules" for such life-and-death decisions remain a major concern.

The issue of accountability also complicates AI decision-making. When a human makes a bad decision, they can be held responsible, face legal consequences, or learn from their mistakes. AI, however, lacks accountability—it cannot experience guilt, learn moral lessons, or take responsibility for harm caused. When an AI-driven system makes an unfair hiring decision, denies someone a loan, or misdiagnoses a patient, who is to blame? The programmer? The company deploying the AI? The AI itself? The lack of clear accountability makes ethical oversight of AI-driven decision-making even more difficult.

Despite these challenges, some researchers believe that AI can be programmed to follow ethical principles by incorporating ethical reasoning frameworks into algorithms. Efforts are being made to create AI systems that can recognize moral dilemmas, balance competing values, and make decisions that align with societal norms. However, AI's inability to "understand" ethics in the way humans do means that even the most advanced ethical AI will still operate based on predefined rules rather than true moral reasoning.

To bridge the gap between human morality and machine decision-making, strong regulatory frameworks, transparency, and human oversight are essential. AI should be designed as a tool that assists human decision-making rather than replacing it in ethically complex scenarios. Governments, businesses, and researchers must work together to ensure AI systems are fair, explainable, and accountable.

In conclusion, while AI can be trained to follow ethical guidelines, it will never possess true moral reasoning, intuition, or emotional understanding. Machine decision-making is fundamentally different from human ethics, and without proper oversight, it risks creating a world where decisions are made based on optimization rather than justice, empathy, or fairness. The challenge is not just about making AI more ethical—it is about ensuring that human values remain central in an increasingly automated world.

The Role of AI in Law and Justice

Artificial Intelligence (AI) is transforming the legal and judicial systems, bringing efficiency, automation, and data-driven decision-making to an industry historically reliant on human expertise. From automating document review and legal research to assisting in court rulings and predictive analytics, AI is reshaping how legal professionals work and how justice is administered. While AI presents significant advantages in terms of efficiency and accessibility, it also raises ethical and legal concerns, including bias in decision-making, accountability, and the potential erosion of human judgment in complex legal matters.

One of the most immediate and impactful applications of AI in law is legal research and document analysis. Law firms and legal professionals traditionally spend hours sifting through vast amounts of case law, contracts, and legal precedents to build arguments and prepare cases. AI-powered legal research tools, such as ROSS Intelligence and Westlaw Edge, use natural language processing (NLP) to quickly analyze legal texts, identify relevant precedents, and provide case summaries. This significantly reduces the time and cost associated with legal research, allowing lawyers to focus on higher-level strategic tasks rather than manual document review.

Another key application of AI in law is contract analysis and automation. Businesses and law firms deal with thousands of contracts that require careful examination to identify risks, obligations, and compliance requirements. AI-powered contract management systems can automatically review and extract important clauses, detect inconsistencies, and flag potential legal risks. By streamlining contract analysis, AI reduces human error and ensures legal compliance, particularly in industries such as finance, healthcare, and real estate, where regulatory requirements are complex and constantly evolving.

AI is also playing an increasingly prominent role in predictive analytics for legal decision-making. By analyzing historical case data, AI can predict case outcomes, assess the likelihood of success for specific legal arguments, and even provide insights into judicial tendencies. For example, AI models can analyze past rulings by judges to determine how they may rule in similar cases in the future. Law firms and clients can use these insights to make informed decisions about whether to settle, proceed to trial, or adjust legal strategies. However, predictive justice raises ethical concerns—if AI relies on biased historical data, it may reinforce systemic injustices and disadvantage marginalized groups.

In the judicial system, AI is being used to support court proceedings and decision-making. Some jurisdictions are experimenting with AI-powered sentencing recommendations, bail assessments, and risk assessment tools. AI-driven systems like COMPAS (Correctional Offender Management Profiling for Alternative Sanctions) have been used to predict the likelihood of reoffending, assisting judges in determining appropriate sentences and parole decisions. However, studies have shown that AI models can reflect and amplify racial and socio-economic biases present in historical judicial data. When AI-based systems predict recidivism rates or assess bail eligibility, they may disproportionately impact minority communities, raising concerns about fairness and due process.

Another critical area where AI is making a difference is legal accessibility and dispute resolution. Many people, especially those with limited financial resources, struggle to access legal assistance. AI-powered legal chatbots and virtual assistants, such as DoNotPay, provide free or low-cost legal guidance, helping individuals contest parking tickets, navigate landlord-tenant disputes, or understand consumer rights. AI-driven online dispute resolution platforms also help resolve conflicts outside of traditional court settings, making legal assistance more accessible to those who cannot afford traditional legal representation.

Despite the advantages AI brings to the legal and judicial systems, significant challenges remain. One of the biggest concerns is accountability and liability—if an AI system provides incorrect legal advice or makes biased sentencing recommendations, who is responsible? Legal professionals and judges rely on human reasoning, ethical considerations, and contextual judgment— qualities AI lacks. Moreover, AI operates as a "black box" in many cases, making it difficult to understand how decisions are made, further complicating transparency and accountability.

There is also the issue of privacy and data security. Legal cases often involve highly sensitive information, and AI-driven legal tools rely on vast datasets to train their algorithms. Ensuring that client confidentiality and data privacy are maintained is crucial, especially as AI adoption in the legal sector continues to grow. Strong data governance frameworks and regulations must be in place to prevent misuse of sensitive legal data.

To ensure AI's ethical and effective integration into the legal system, governments, legal institutions, and AI developers must collaborate to create robust regulatory frameworks. AI should be used as an assistive tool rather than a replacement for human judgment, with clear guidelines on transparency, accountability, and fairness. Regular audits of AI systems must be conducted to detect and correct biases, ensuring that AI serves justice rather than distorting it.

In conclusion, AI is playing an increasingly influential role in law and justice, offering benefits such as efficiency, cost reduction, and improved access to legal resources. However, it also poses ethical and legal challenges that must be carefully addressed. The future of AI in the legal system depends on striking the right balance between technological advancement and human oversight, ensuring that AI enhances, rather than undermines, the fundamental principles of justice.

AI Ethics Boards and Global Regulations

AI ethics boards and global regulations are becoming increasingly essential as artificial intelligence continues to expand its influence across industries and societies. AI systems now make critical decisions in areas such as healthcare, finance, law enforcement, and national security. However, the rapid growth of AI has outpaced regulatory efforts, leading to concerns over bias, accountability, transparency, and the ethical implications of its widespread adoption. Governments, corporations, and research institutions are recognizing the need for structured oversight to ensure that AI development aligns with fundamental human rights and societal values.

AI ethics boards have emerged as a mechanism to oversee the responsible development and deployment of AI technologies. These boards are typically composed of experts from diverse fields, including ethics, law, computer science, and public policy. Their primary function is to establish guidelines that promote fairness, transparency, and accountability in AI decision-making. Ethics boards review AI applications to ensure that they do not reinforce discrimination, violate privacy rights, or pose risks to public safety. They also provide recommendations on how AI systems can be designed and implemented to align with ethical principles. Some major technology companies, including Google, Microsoft, and IBM, have established internal AI ethics boards to self-regulate their AI projects. However, critics argue that industry-led ethics boards may lack the impartiality needed to hold corporations accountable, as financial and competitive interests could influence their decisions. Independent ethics boards formed by governments and global institutions are seen as a more effective way to enforce ethical AI practices.

Despite the growing presence of ethics boards, AI regulation remains a fragmented and complex issue. Different countries have varying approaches to AI governance, creating inconsistencies in how AI is developed and used. The European Union has taken the lead in AI regulation with the introduction of the AI Act, which classifies AI systems based on risk levels and imposes strict requirements on high-risk applications such as facial recognition and predictive policing. The United Nations has also formed AI advisory groups to develop ethical guidelines that prioritize human rights, data privacy, and security. The OECD has established global AI principles aimed at promoting fairness and accountability in AI adoption. However, global AI regulation is complicated by geopolitical tensions, as leading AI powers like the United States and China have different priorities when it comes to AI development. The U.S. has largely focused on innovation and economic competitiveness, while China has implemented stringent AI regulations, particularly in areas related to surveillance and content moderation. The lack of a unified regulatory framework makes it difficult to establish global AI standards that balance technological progress with ethical concerns.

One of the greatest challenges in AI regulation is defining ethical AI in a universally accepted way. Ethics are subjective, and different cultures, legal systems, and political ideologies influence how AI is perceived and governed. Another challenge is balancing regulation with innovation, as excessive restrictions could slow AI development and limit its potential benefits. AI technologies evolve rapidly, often outpacing existing laws, making it difficult for regulatory bodies to keep up. Enforcement is also a concern, as some countries may resist adopting international AI regulations, creating loopholes that could allow unethical AI practices to thrive. The risk of AI being weaponized for cyber warfare, misinformation, and mass surveillance further complicates regulatory efforts, highlighting the urgency for coordinated global action.

To ensure that AI serves humanity rather than exploits it, governments, ethics boards, and regulatory bodies must collaborate to establish clear guidelines for responsible AI use. International cooperation is necessary to create standardized policies that ensure AI systems are transparent, fair, and accountable. Regular audits of AI models and their impact on society can help identify biases and ethical risks, allowing for necessary adjustments. AI ethics should not be left solely in the hands of corporations, as public interest groups, legal experts, and independent researchers must also be involved in shaping AI policies. Developers should incorporate ethical considerations into AI systems from the design stage, rather than addressing them as an afterthought.

The future of AI governance will depend on how well regulatory frameworks can keep pace with technological advancements while maintaining ethical integrity. AI ethics boards and global regulations have a critical role in shaping a future where AI enhances human progress rather than exacerbates inequality, privacy violations, and security threats. Without proactive governance, AI could become a tool that deepens social divides and erodes public trust in technology. Effective regulation requires a commitment to upholding human rights, ensuring AI accountability, and fostering an environment where technological innovation benefits all of society. AI is not inherently good or bad; its impact depends on the rules and ethical frameworks that guide its development and deployment. The choices made today will determine whether AI remains a force for good or becomes a tool of unchecked power and exploitation.

Chapter 6
The Surveillance State— Freedom vs. Control

The increasing integration of artificial intelligence into governance and security systems has given rise to a new era of surveillance, where states have unprecedented capabilities to monitor and control their populations. AI-driven surveillance technologies such as facial recognition, biometric tracking, predictive policing, and data aggregation have transformed the way governments enforce laws, maintain public order, and gather intelligence. While proponents argue that these technologies enhance national security, prevent crime, and streamline governance, critics warn of a growing surveillance state that threatens individual freedoms, privacy, and democratic values. The fundamental question facing modern societies is whether AI-powered surveillance serves as a tool for protection or an instrument of control.

Governments across the world have embraced AI-driven surveillance to improve national security and law enforcement. Smart cameras with facial recognition capabilities are now used in cities to track movements, identify individuals, and prevent criminal activities before they happen. Predictive analytics enable law enforcement agencies to analyze vast amounts of data, detecting patterns that help anticipate crimes and threats. AI-powered monitoring systems track online behavior, social media activity, and financial transactions to detect potential security risks. These advancements allow authorities to respond more efficiently to dangers, making surveillance a powerful tool in the fight against terrorism, cybercrime, and organized crime. In authoritarian regimes, however, AI-driven surveillance has been used to suppress dissent, silence opposition voices, and control populations by monitoring political activities, social movements, and even personal interactions.

The erosion of privacy is one of the most significant concerns associated with the rise of AI-driven surveillance. Citizens are increasingly subjected to constant monitoring in public spaces, workplaces, and even their online interactions. AI systems can analyze vast amounts of personal data, from travel habits and purchasing behavior to medical records and private communications. In some countries, social credit systems have been implemented, where individuals are scored based on their behaviors, financial transactions, and social interactions. Those who fail to comply with state-approved behavior face restrictions on their ability to travel, access services, or secure employment. This level of surveillance blurs the lines between security and control, raising ethical and human rights concerns.

The expansion of surveillance capabilities also raises issues of accountability and oversight. AI systems operate with minimal human intervention, making it difficult to challenge or correct false identifications and biased decisions. Facial recognition algorithms, for example, have been criticized for racial and gender biases, leading to wrongful arrests and discrimination. The lack of transparency in how AI surveillance systems are designed and deployed means that individuals often have no way of knowing when or how they are being monitored. Without legal safeguards, AI-powered surveillance risks becoming an unchecked force that undermines civil liberties.

Balancing security with personal freedom requires robust legal frameworks, ethical guidelines, and public discourse on the limits of surveillance. Governments must ensure that AI surveillance systems are used responsibly, with clear regulations that prevent misuse and protect individuals' rights. Citizens must have the ability to challenge wrongful surveillance and seek legal recourse when their privacy is violated. Technology companies that develop AI-driven surveillance tools also bear responsibility in ensuring that their technologies are not weaponized for oppression.

The debate over AI surveillance represents a fundamental struggle between freedom and control. In democratic societies, AI can be leveraged to improve public safety without infringing on civil liberties, but in the wrong hands, it can become a tool for totalitarian control. How governments and societies choose to regulate and implement AI surveillance will determine whether it remains a tool for protection or becomes a mechanism for unchecked authoritarianism. The choices made today will shape the future of privacy, security, and human rights in the AI-driven world.

AI in Policing and Predictive Crime Analytics

Artificial intelligence is increasingly being integrated into law enforcement, with police departments worldwide adopting AI-driven technologies to enhance crime prevention, improve public safety, and optimize resource allocation. AI in policing and predictive crime analytics promises to make law enforcement more efficient, allowing officers to anticipate criminal activity, identify suspects, and allocate resources more effectively. However, the deployment of AI in policing also raises ethical concerns about privacy, bias, accountability, and the potential for mass surveillance. While AI-driven crime prediction may offer benefits in reducing crime rates, its application must be carefully managed to prevent discrimination, wrongful accusations, and the erosion of civil liberties.

One of the most common uses of AI in policing is predictive crime analytics, which uses historical crime data, geographic mapping, and machine learning algorithms to forecast where crimes are most likely to occur. By analyzing past incidents, AI can identify crime hotspots and suggest areas where increased police presence may be necessary. This data-driven approach allows law enforcement agencies to allocate patrols more efficiently, focusing on high-risk locations rather than relying solely on traditional policing instincts. AI-powered crime mapping tools have been adopted by several major cities, helping police forces optimize their deployment of officers and reduce response times to criminal activity.

Facial recognition technology is another AI-driven tool widely used in law enforcement. AI-powered surveillance cameras equipped with facial recognition software can scan and identify individuals in real time, matching their faces against databases of criminal records, missing persons, or wanted fugitives. This technology has been instrumental in locating suspects, enhancing security at public events, and identifying individuals involved in criminal activities. However, facial recognition has been heavily criticized for its inaccuracies, particularly when identifying people of color. Studies have shown that some facial recognition algorithms have higher error rates when analyzing non-white faces, leading to concerns about wrongful arrests and racial profiling. The potential for misidentification and discriminatory enforcement has prompted calls for stricter regulations on the use of facial recognition in policing.

AI is also being used to analyze digital evidence, automate forensic investigations, and assist in criminal profiling. AI-powered forensic tools can examine vast amounts of digital data, including emails, phone records, and social media activity, to detect suspicious behavior and uncover patterns linked to criminal activity. Machine learning algorithms can also assist in criminal profiling by analyzing behavioral data and identifying characteristics that may indicate a suspect's likelihood of reoffending. AI-driven surveillance systems monitor online platforms for signs of illegal activities, such as human trafficking, drug transactions, and cybercrime. While these applications can enhance law enforcement capabilities, they also raise concerns about mass surveillance and potential violations of privacy rights.

One of the most controversial aspects of AI in policing is its role in predictive policing programs, where AI algorithms analyze data to predict potential criminals before a crime is committed. These systems assess individuals based on their past behavior, social interactions, and demographic factors, assigning risk scores that law enforcement agencies may use to prioritize investigations or surveillance. While predictive policing aims to prevent crime before it happens, critics argue that it disproportionately targets marginalized communities, reinforcing systemic biases in the criminal justice system. Because AI models are trained on historical crime data, they often inherit and amplify existing prejudices, leading to over-policing in certain neighborhoods and increased scrutiny of specific demographic groups.

Another ethical concern surrounding AI in policing is the issue of accountability. AI-driven decisions can influence arrests, sentencing, and law enforcement actions, yet AI systems themselves cannot be held responsible for errors or biases. When AI makes a mistake, such as falsely identifying an innocent person as a suspect, it is often difficult to determine who is accountable—the software developers, the police officers using the technology, or the agency that implemented the system. This lack of clear accountability creates legal and ethical challenges, highlighting the need for greater transparency and oversight in AI-driven policing.

To address these concerns, governments and law enforcement agencies must establish regulations that ensure AI in policing is used responsibly and ethically. Transparency in AI decision-making, regular audits of policing algorithms, and mechanisms for individuals to challenge AI-driven decisions are essential to maintaining public trust. AI should serve as a tool to assist law enforcement rather than replace human judgment, ensuring that officers retain the responsibility of evaluating each case on its merits rather than blindly following algorithmic recommendations.

While AI has the potential to enhance policing and crime prevention, its implementation must be approached with caution. If used responsibly, AI-driven crime analytics can improve public safety, reduce crime rates, and optimize law enforcement efforts. However, without proper safeguards, AI could lead to wrongful accusations, racial discrimination, and the erosion of civil liberties. The future of AI in policing will depend on striking a balance between technological innovation and the protection of fundamental human rights, ensuring that law enforcement agencies use AI as a tool for justice rather than an instrument of oppression.

China's Social Credit System: A Glimpse into the Future?

China's Social Credit System is one of the most ambitious and controversial applications of artificial intelligence-driven surveillance and behavioral monitoring in the modern world. Designed as a nationwide initiative to assess the trustworthiness of individuals, businesses, and even government entities, the system integrates vast amounts of personal data to generate a score that determines privileges and restrictions in various aspects of life. This AI-powered framework represents a potential model for future governance, raising profound ethical and human rights concerns about privacy, personal freedom, and state control. While China's government promotes the system as a way to enhance societal trust, improve compliance with laws, and create a more harmonious society, critics warn that it represents a dystopian vision of mass surveillance and authoritarian control.

The Social Credit System works by collecting and analyzing data from multiple sources, including financial transactions, social behavior, legal records, and even personal interactions. Citizens are scored based on their compliance with government policies, social responsibility, and financial reliability. Positive behaviors, such as paying bills on time, volunteering, or engaging in government-approved activities, can lead to higher scores and access to benefits, including better loan conditions, priority access to services, and travel privileges. Conversely, negative behaviors—such as spreading misinformation, failing to pay debts, engaging in protests, or even associating with individuals considered "untrustworthy"—can result in penalties. These penalties can include travel restrictions, exclusion from high-paying jobs, slower internet speeds, and social stigmatization. Some reports suggest that individuals with low scores may also face difficulties renting apartments, enrolling their children in preferred schools, or accessing certain public services.

A key component of China's Social Credit System is its reliance on artificial intelligence, big data, and facial recognition technology. AI-powered surveillance cameras track people's movements, biometric identification systems verify identities, and algorithms analyze behaviors in real time. AI plays a crucial role in monitoring financial transactions, online activity, and public interactions, allowing the government to maintain an unprecedented level of oversight. The system also incorporates public reporting mechanisms, where citizens can report unethical behavior, further incentivizing compliance and reinforcing government control. This level of interconnected data collection and AI-driven analysis enables the government to enforce social norms and suppress dissent more efficiently than traditional law enforcement methods.

One of the most concerning aspects of the Social Credit System is its potential for misuse and the erosion of personal freedoms. Unlike traditional financial credit scores, which primarily assess economic trustworthiness, China's system extends into moral and political territory, influencing personal behavior and ideological alignment. The lack of transparency in how scores are calculated and the absence of a clear appeals process leave citizens vulnerable to arbitrary or politically motivated punishments. The system's design also raises fears that AI-powered governance could be exported to other countries, especially as China continues to develop AI technologies for international use. Some governments and corporations have shown interest in adopting similar models for security and behavioral tracking, sparking concerns that AI-driven social control could become a global trend.

The implications of China's Social Credit System go beyond domestic governance, influencing international debates on surveillance, privacy, and digital authoritarianism. While some argue that elements of social credit scoring could be beneficial in promoting accountability and lawfulness, the risks associated with AI-powered social control far outweigh the benefits. If similar systems were to be adopted on a wider scale, they could fundamentally alter the relationship between individuals and the state, creating societies where personal freedoms are dictated by AI-driven algorithms rather than democratic principles.

Ultimately, China's Social Credit System provides a glimpse into a possible future where artificial intelligence plays a central role in shaping human behavior, governance, and societal structure. The world must carefully consider the ethical and human rights consequences of such AI-driven social engineering. If left unchecked, AI-based social control could become the defining governance model of the 21st century, challenging the fundamental values of privacy, autonomy, and individual rights. The debate surrounding China's Social Credit System serves as a warning about the potential dangers of AI-powered surveillance and underscores the urgent need for ethical AI regulations that prioritize human dignity and freedom over algorithmic compliance and control.

The Dilemma of Data: Who Owns Your Information?

The rapid expansion of artificial intelligence and digital technologies has led to an explosion of data collection, raising a critical question: who owns your information? From personal details shared on social media to financial transactions, health records, and location tracking, individuals generate vast amounts of data every day. This data is collected, analyzed, and monetized by corporations, governments, and tech giants, often without explicit consent or full transparency. As AI-driven systems rely on vast datasets to improve algorithms and make predictions, the ownership, control, and ethical implications of data usage have become central concerns. The dilemma of data ownership is more than just a privacy issue—it is about power, control, and the future of digital rights.

The dominant business model of the internet is built on data extraction, with tech companies such as Google, Facebook, Amazon, and Apple collecting enormous amounts of user information. In exchange for free services, users unknowingly "pay" with their personal data, which is used to target advertisements, predict consumer behavior, and refine AI algorithms. Data is now considered the most valuable commodity in the digital age, often referred to as the "new oil." However, unlike traditional commodities, data is generated by individuals, raising the ethical question of whether users should have ownership rights over their personal information. Most people have little control over how their data is collected, shared, and sold, leading to concerns about exploitation and misuse.

Governments also play a significant role in data collection, often using AI-powered surveillance systems to monitor citizens. National security agencies, law enforcement, and intelligence organizations track digital footprints to prevent crimes, combat terrorism, and enforce public policies. However, this level of data collection raises concerns about mass surveillance, privacy invasion, and the erosion of civil liberties. In some cases, governments partner with private tech firms to gain access to large datasets, blurring the lines between corporate and state control of information. This raises fundamental questions about accountability and whether individuals can truly own their data when both private entities and government institutions have unrestricted access to it.

The issue of data ownership becomes even more complicated when considering how AI systems use personal information. AI models are trained on vast datasets, often without individuals' knowledge or explicit consent. Facial recognition technology, for example, relies on millions of images scraped from the internet, many of which were uploaded by users who never agreed to their faces being used for AI training. Similarly, AI-generated text, images, and music often draw from publicly available content, raising concerns about copyright, intellectual property, and fair compensation for content creators. The dilemma extends to biometric data, medical records, and genetic information, where companies developing AI-driven healthcare solutions may claim ownership of patient data, raising ethical and legal questions.

In response to these concerns, governments and regulatory bodies have introduced data protection laws to give individuals more control over their personal information. The General Data Protection Regulation (GDPR) in the European Union is one of the most comprehensive data protection laws, requiring companies to obtain user consent before collecting data and allowing individuals to request deletion of their personal information. Similarly, the California Consumer Privacy Act (CCPA) grants users more transparency and control over how their data is used. However, these regulations are still evolving, and enforcement remains a challenge, especially as AI-driven data collection becomes more sophisticated.

Despite legal protections, the fundamental imbalance in data ownership remains unresolved. Users continue to generate data, but corporations and governments remain the primary beneficiaries. Some experts have proposed alternative models to redistribute control over personal data, such as data trusts, where independent organizations manage and safeguard personal data on behalf of individuals. Others advocate for a personal data economy, where users could sell or license their own data, allowing them to benefit financially from the information they generate. Blockchain technology has also been suggested as a potential solution, providing decentralized and transparent mechanisms for individuals to control access to their data.

The dilemma of data ownership is not just about privacy—it is about power in the digital age. If individuals do not have control over their own information, they risk becoming passive participants in a system where AI, corporations, and governments dictate the rules. The question of who owns your data is ultimately a question about digital rights, ethical AI development, and the need for a fairer and more transparent approach to data governance. Without meaningful reforms, the current trajectory could lead to an AI-driven future where personal information is exploited for profit and control, rather than being treated as a fundamental right of every individual.

Balancing Security and Civil Liberties in an AI World

The rise of artificial intelligence in security, law enforcement, and governance has brought unprecedented capabilities to prevent crime, detect threats, and protect public safety. AI-driven surveillance, predictive policing, and automated decision-making have enabled authorities to respond to potential risks faster than ever before. However, as AI becomes more deeply integrated into security frameworks, it presents a fundamental challenge: how can societies balance safety with the protection of civil liberties? The tension between national security and individual freedoms has long existed, but AI's ability to process vast amounts of data, monitor populations in real time, and make autonomous decisions raises concerns about privacy, fairness, and accountability.

AI-powered security systems rely on advanced technologies such as facial recognition, biometric tracking, and real-time data analysis to identify potential threats. Governments and private entities deploy these tools in airports, public spaces, and border security to enhance safety. Predictive analytics help law enforcement agencies anticipate crime hotspots, while AI-powered surveillance networks assist in identifying individuals linked to criminal activities. In the private sector, AI is used to detect fraud, cybersecurity threats, and suspicious financial transactions. Proponents argue that AI enhances security by reducing human error, increasing efficiency, and enabling proactive intervention before crimes or attacks occur. AI-driven threat detection systems have played a crucial role in counterterrorism, helping governments track illicit activities and prevent large-scale security breaches.

However, the widespread use of AI in security comes at a cost: the erosion of civil liberties. The most pressing concern is mass surveillance, where AI-powered cameras, sensors, and digital tracking create a system of constant monitoring. Facial recognition technology, for instance, allows governments to track individuals without their knowledge or consent. In some countries, AI-powered surveillance has been used to monitor political dissidents, restrict freedom of expression, and suppress protests. Even in democratic societies, the expansion of AI-driven security measures raises fears that governments may use technology to justify authoritarian control under the guise of public safety.

Another major concern is the lack of transparency and accountability in AI-driven security decisions. AI algorithms operate based on complex machine learning models, often referred to as "black boxes," where even developers may not fully understand how an AI system reaches a particular decision. When AI makes mistakes—such as falsely identifying innocent individuals as security threats—who is responsible? The opacity of AI decision-making makes it difficult for individuals to challenge unfair or biased security measures. Studies have shown that some facial recognition systems have higher error rates for people of color, leading to wrongful detentions and racial profiling. Without strict oversight, AI security tools risk reinforcing systemic discrimination and violating human rights.

The question of how to balance security with civil liberties in an AI world is ultimately one of governance. Governments must establish legal frameworks that regulate the use of AI in security while protecting individual freedoms. Transparency measures, such as requiring AI systems to be explainable and auditable, can help ensure that AI-driven security decisions are fair and accountable. Clear regulations should define how AI surveillance is used, who has access to collected data, and how individuals can contest AI-based decisions that affect them. Independent oversight bodies should be established to review AI security programs, ensuring they do not infringe upon civil liberties.

Another critical solution lies in public engagement and democratic participation. Citizens must have a voice in shaping AI security policies, ensuring that they align with ethical principles and human rights. Open discussions on the implications of AI-driven security, privacy rights, and the scope of government surveillance are necessary to strike a balance between protection and personal freedom. Technology companies also bear responsibility in designing AI systems that prioritize privacy and ethical considerations, rather than simply maximizing security at the cost of individual rights.

The challenge of balancing security and civil liberties in an AI world is not just a legal or technological issue—it is a question of societal values. While AI has the potential to enhance safety, it must not come at the expense of fundamental freedoms. Striking the right balance requires thoughtful regulation, ethical AI development, and ongoing public dialogue to ensure that AI serves as a tool for protection rather than oppression. If left unchecked, AI-driven security could lead to a world where privacy is a privilege rather than a right, fundamentally altering the relationship between individuals and the state. The decisions made today will shape the future of both security and democracy in an AI-powered world.

Chapter 7
The AI Arms Race—A Battle for Superintelligence

The rapid advancement of artificial intelligence has ignited an intense global competition among nations, corporations, and research institutions, all vying to achieve breakthroughs in AI that could redefine economic power, military strength, and technological supremacy. This escalating race, often referred to as the AI arms race, is not merely about developing smarter algorithms or automating industries—it is about the pursuit of superintelligence, a level of AI that surpasses human cognitive abilities in nearly every domain. Governments and corporations alike recognize that whoever leads in AI development will hold unparalleled strategic advantages, influencing global affairs, security, and economic dominance in the decades to come.

At the heart of this competition are two of the world's largest powers: the United States and China. Both nations have heavily invested in AI research, military applications, and economic strategies driven by artificial intelligence. China's government has made AI a central part of its national strategy, aiming to become the global leader in AI by 2030. With state-backed funding, an immense population generating vast amounts of training data, and AI-driven surveillance systems already in place, China has positioned itself as a formidable force in AI development. The United States, meanwhile, has long been at the forefront of AI research, with companies like

Google, OpenAI, Microsoft, and IBM pushing the boundaries of machine learning, robotics, and autonomous systems. Silicon Valley remains a dominant hub of AI innovation, attracting top researchers and talent from around the world. This competition has been described as a new form of Cold War—one fought not with nuclear weapons but with algorithms, computing power, and data superiority.

The military implications of AI supremacy are a key driver of the AI arms race. Autonomous drones, AI-powered cyber warfare, and robotic soldiers are no longer concepts confined to science fiction. Nations are developing AI-driven weapons systems capable of analyzing battle conditions, identifying enemy targets, and making strategic decisions faster than human commanders. AI-enhanced cyber warfare presents an even more immediate threat, where nations use AI to launch cyberattacks, manipulate digital infrastructure, and infiltrate critical systems. The integration of AI into defense strategies has led to concerns about lethal autonomous weapons, often referred to as "killer robots," which could make life-or-death decisions without human oversight. Ethical concerns surrounding AI in warfare have prompted debates over whether these technologies should be regulated or banned altogether.

Beyond military applications, the AI arms race extends to economic and technological supremacy. AI-driven automation is revolutionizing industries, from manufacturing and finance to healthcare and transportation. The country or corporation that dominates AI-driven economic models could control the future of global trade, digital currencies, and technological infrastructure. Companies are in a fierce competition to develop AI that can optimize supply chains, predict financial trends, and even create AI-generated content for media and entertainment. The race for quantum computing and AI integration adds another layer of complexity, as quantum AI has the potential to process information exponentially faster than traditional computing, giving its developers an unprecedented advantage in research, security, and economic forecasting.

However, the pursuit of superintelligence carries significant risks. The fear of AI surpassing human control, making unpredictable decisions, or acting against human interests has raised existential concerns. Leading AI researchers have warned about the potential dangers of developing AI that can improve itself beyond human understanding, potentially leading to unintended consequences. Without international agreements on AI ethics, governance, and safety protocols, the AI arms race could spiral into a scenario where nations and corporations recklessly push the boundaries of AI capabilities without considering the long-term consequences.

The AI arms race is not just a geopolitical contest—it is a defining challenge of the 21st century that will shape the future of warfare, governance, and civilization itself. The world must decide whether AI will be developed as a tool for cooperation, shared progress, and ethical advancement, or whether it will become a battleground for technological supremacy, economic domination, and uncontrolled risks. The decisions made in the coming years will determine whether AI becomes humanity's greatest ally or its most unpredictable adversary.

The Race for AGI (Artificial General Intelligence)

The pursuit of Artificial General Intelligence (AGI) represents one of the most ambitious and consequential scientific endeavors of the 21st century. Unlike narrow AI, which excels in specific tasks such as language translation, facial recognition, or autonomous driving,

AGI refers to a system with human-like intelligence, capable of reasoning, learning, and adapting across multiple domains without being confined to predefined functions. Achieving AGI would mark a revolutionary shift in technology, potentially surpassing human cognitive abilities in nearly every field. Governments, corporations, and research institutions around the world are engaged in a competitive race to develop AGI, driven by the promise of unlocking unprecedented economic, military, and societal advantages. However, the path to AGI is fraught with technical, ethical, and existential challenges, raising profound questions about control, safety, and the long-term consequences of creating a machine intelligence that rivals human intellect.

The leading players in the AGI race include technology giants such as OpenAI, Google DeepMind, Meta, and Microsoft, along with major research institutions and government-backed initiatives. OpenAI, for instance, has publicly stated its mission to build AGI that benefits all of humanity, advocating for careful and ethical development. DeepMind, a subsidiary of Alphabet (Google's parent company), has made groundbreaking advancements in AI, including AlphaGo and AlphaFold, demonstrating AI's potential to master complex problems. Meanwhile, China has heavily invested in AI and AGI research, aiming to establish itself as a global leader in artificial intelligence by 2030. The rivalry between the U.S. and China in AGI development mirrors the geopolitical competition seen in other areas of AI, such as cybersecurity, automation, and military technology.

The technological foundation for AGI is built on machine learning, deep neural networks, reinforcement learning, and massive computational power. Current AI models, such as GPT-4, exhibit impressive language comprehension and reasoning abilities, but they still lack true general intelligence—the ability to understand context, learn from minimal data, and apply knowledge flexibly across different domains. To achieve AGI, researchers are exploring self-improving AI, where machines enhance their own capabilities without direct human intervention. The integration of brain-inspired computing, neuromorphic chips, and quantum computing is also being considered as potential breakthroughs that could accelerate AGI development.

While the race for AGI is driven by the promise of economic transformation and scientific discovery, it also presents serious risks and ethical dilemmas. If AGI surpasses human intelligence and becomes capable of recursive self-improvement, it could rapidly evolve beyond human control. This scenario, often referred to as the intelligence explosion, raises concerns about AI alignment—ensuring that AGI's goals and behaviors remain aligned with human values. Without proper safeguards, AGI could prioritize objectives that are misaligned with human well-being, leading to unintended or catastrophic consequences. The prospect of AGI being weaponized for cyber warfare, mass surveillance, or autonomous military systems further complicates the ethical landscape.

One of the biggest challenges in AGI development is ensuring global cooperation and responsible governance. The absence of international regulations or agreements on AGI research creates an environment where nations and corporations are incentivized to push forward at any cost, potentially disregarding safety precautions in the pursuit of competitive advantage. Calls for AGI safety research, ethical AI principles, and regulatory oversight have been growing, with prominent AI researchers warning about the potential dangers of uncontrolled AGI development. Some experts advocate for a global coalition similar to nuclear arms treaties, ensuring that AGI research is conducted with transparency and shared safety protocols.

Despite these concerns, the potential benefits of AGI are staggering. If developed responsibly, AGI could solve some of humanity's greatest challenges, from accelerating medical research and curing diseases to addressing climate change and optimizing global economic systems. AGI could revolutionize space exploration, automate scientific discovery, and usher in an era of post-scarcity where intelligent systems handle labor-intensive tasks, freeing humans to pursue creative and intellectual endeavors. However, realizing this optimistic future requires a deliberate and cautious approach, ensuring that AGI development prioritizes ethical considerations over competition and unchecked ambition.

The race for AGI is more than just a technological contest—it is a defining moment in human history that will shape the future of civilization. The decisions made today will determine whether AGI emerges as humanity's greatest ally or its most formidable challenge. The need for ethical foresight, responsible innovation, and international collaboration has never been greater. AGI has the potential to reshape the world in ways that were once only imagined in science fiction, but without careful governance, it could also lead to unforeseen consequences beyond human control. The balance between ambition and caution will ultimately decide whether AGI leads to a golden age of progress or a future fraught with existential risk.

AI as a Tool of Geopolitical Dominance

Artificial intelligence has emerged as a powerful tool for geopolitical dominance, reshaping global power structures, influencing economic policies, and redefining military strategies. Nations that lead in AI development gain a strategic edge in warfare, economic competition, cybersecurity, and global influence, making

AI one of the most contested technological frontiers in modern history. The race for AI supremacy is not just about innovation—it is about control, national security, and the ability to shape the future of global governance. As AI becomes increasingly integrated into defense, surveillance, trade, and diplomacy, the geopolitical landscape is undergoing a transformation where technological superiority determines political power.

At the heart of this AI-driven geopolitical competition are the United States and China, the two dominant forces investing heavily in artificial intelligence research, military applications, and AI-driven economies. China has explicitly stated its ambition to become the world leader in AI by 2030, embedding AI into its national strategy to enhance governance, economic growth, and military capabilities. The Chinese government has invested billions into AI-driven infrastructure, mass surveillance, and predictive policing, while state-backed firms like Huawei and Tencent are expanding AI-powered technologies globally. By integrating AI into its Belt and Road Initiative, China is not only advancing its own technological ecosystem but also exporting AI-driven surveillance tools to other nations, extending its influence beyond its borders.

The United States, on the other hand, maintains a strong foothold in AI research and development, largely due to private sector dominance. Silicon Valley giants such as Google, OpenAI, Microsoft, and IBM are at the forefront of AI innovation, advancing breakthroughs in machine learning, natural language processing, and autonomous systems. The U.S. government has recognized AI as a critical component of national security, leading to increased military investments in AI-powered cyber defense, drone warfare, and autonomous battlefield technologies. The Pentagon's AI-driven initiatives, such as Project Maven, focus on using machine learning to analyze vast amounts of surveillance data, identifying threats more efficiently than human analysts. However, unlike China's state-controlled AI approach, the U.S. operates in a decentralized model where private tech firms play a significant role in AI development.

Beyond the U.S. and China, other global players are investing in AI for strategic and economic leverage. The European Union has prioritized ethical AI governance and regulation, focusing on maintaining democratic values while remaining competitive in AI-driven industries. Russia has emphasized AI in military applications, particularly in autonomous weapons and cyber warfare, positioning AI as a key component of modern warfare strategies. Meanwhile, countries like India, Japan, and South Korea are emerging as AI hubs, leveraging AI for economic growth, healthcare, and smart city development.

AI's role in cyber warfare and information control has further intensified global competition. AI-driven cyberattacks, deepfake propaganda, and misinformation campaigns are increasingly used by state actors to manipulate public opinion, disrupt elections, and weaken geopolitical rivals. Governments and intelligence agencies are using AI to detect and counter cyber threats, but the offensive use of AI in disinformation warfare is an escalating concern. As AI-generated fake news and deepfake videos become more convincing, the risk of political destabilization and digital warfare grows, making AI an essential component of modern intelligence operations.

Another key area where AI is influencing geopolitical power is economic control and trade dominance. AI-driven automation is transforming industries, reducing labor costs, and reshaping supply chains. Countries with advanced AI capabilities can optimize manufacturing, predict financial trends, and dominate AI-driven economic sectors, giving them a competitive advantage in global trade. AI is also at the center of semiconductor production and chip manufacturing, with nations recognizing that control over AI hardware is just as important as AI software. The U.S. has imposed restrictions on semiconductor exports to China, aiming to limit China's ability to develop cutting-edge AI technologies without reliance on American chip manufacturers.

The global AI arms race has also raised concerns about AI ethics, governance, and regulation. Without international agreements on AI safety and responsible development, AI could be weaponized for oppressive surveillance, autonomous warfare, and cyber espionage. The absence of universal AI laws makes it easier for authoritarian regimes to use AI for mass surveillance, social control, and suppression of dissent, further complicating global diplomatic relations. Organizations such as the United Nations and the European Union have called for AI regulations, but enforcement remains a challenge as different countries pursue AI development based on their own political agendas.

AI is not just a technological revolution—it is a geopolitical force that is reshaping global power dynamics. The ability to develop, deploy, and regulate AI will determine which nations emerge as leaders in the digital age and which ones fall behind. As AI continues to evolve, governments must balance technological ambition with ethical responsibility, ensuring that AI is used for global stability rather than as a tool for conflict and oppression. The future of AI-driven geopolitics will be shaped by the decisions made today, and those who control AI will ultimately control the future of world power.

The Ethical Risks of Autonomous Weapons

The rise of artificial intelligence in military applications has led to the development of autonomous weapons, AI-driven systems capable of selecting and engaging targets without direct human intervention. These weapons, often referred to as "killer robots," include autonomous drones, robotic soldiers, and AI-powered missile systems that can operate independently on the battlefield. While proponents argue that autonomous weapons could make warfare more efficient, reduce human casualties, and improve precision in military operations, critics warn of serious ethical risks associated with delegating life-and-death decisions to machines. The increasing reliance on AI in combat raises concerns about accountability, the erosion of moral responsibility in warfare, the potential for unintended escalations, and the broader implications of allowing AI to determine the fate of human lives.

One of the most pressing ethical concerns surrounding autonomous weapons is the lack of human oversight in decision-making. Traditional warfare involves soldiers and commanders who exercise judgment, take responsibility for their actions, and are held accountable under international law. Autonomous weapons, however, function based on algorithms that determine when and how to strike, without human intervention in real time. This raises fundamental questions about who is responsible when an autonomous weapon makes a mistake—the military commander who deployed it, the programmer who developed the AI, or the government that authorized its use? Unlike human soldiers, AI lacks the ability to understand the complexities of combat ethics, moral considerations, and the context of specific battlefield situations. This absence of human judgment increases the risk of collateral damage, misidentifications, and unjustified attacks.

Another major ethical issue is the risk of bias and errors in AI targeting systems. Autonomous weapons rely on machine learning algorithms trained on historical combat data, satellite imagery, and sensor inputs to identify and engage targets. However, AI models are only as good as the data they are trained on, and biases in military datasets could lead to flawed decision-making. Studies have shown that facial recognition and pattern-recognition AI often misidentify individuals based on racial and gender biases, raising the concern that autonomous weapons could disproportionately target specific ethnic or civilian groups. Unlike human soldiers, who can evaluate a situation holistically, AI may misinterpret data and mistakenly classify civilians as combatants, leading to wrongful deaths.

The use of autonomous weapons also increases the risk of unintended escalation and warfare proliferation. Unlike conventional weapons, AI-powered combat systems can operate at speeds far beyond human reaction time. If multiple nations deploy autonomous weapons with minimal oversight, AI-driven conflicts could escalate rapidly, potentially triggering unintended wars or large-scale destruction before human intervention can stop them. The integration of AI into military decision-making also opens the possibility of hacked or malfunctioning AI systems, which could lead to unintended attacks on friendly forces or civilian populations. The potential for AI-driven cyber warfare, where autonomous weapons are hijacked or reprogrammed by adversarial nations or terrorist groups, adds another layer of complexity and danger.

Another significant concern is the moral and legal accountability of autonomous weapons under international humanitarian law. Current legal frameworks, such as the Geneva Conventions, were designed to regulate human-led warfare, ensuring that military actions adhere to principles of distinction, proportionality, and necessity. However, existing laws do not adequately address the unique challenges posed by AI-driven weapons, particularly regarding how responsibility is assigned for war crimes committed by autonomous systems. If an autonomous weapon violates international law by targeting civilians or engaging in indiscriminate attacks, prosecuting its actions under traditional legal systems becomes nearly impossible, as no single individual may be directly responsible for the decision.

The potential for autonomous weapons to be used in authoritarian regimes, extrajudicial killings, and oppressive surveillance states is another alarming ethical risk. Unlike traditional military hardware, autonomous weapons can be programmed for targeted assassinations, political suppression, and mass surveillance without oversight from independent judicial or ethical bodies. Governments could deploy AI-powered drones to eliminate dissidents, journalists, or activists, creating a world where state-sanctioned violence is carried out with minimal accountability. This would set a dangerous precedent where life-and-death decisions are removed from human hands and placed entirely in the control of AI-driven warfare.

Despite these concerns, military investments in autonomous weapons are accelerating, with leading nations such as the United States, China, Russia, and Israel developing AI-powered combat systems. While some international organizations and activists have called for a global ban on fully autonomous weapons, similar to past efforts to ban chemical and biological weapons, no binding international treaty currently restricts their development or deployment. The United Nations and human rights organizations have urged for greater oversight, but without collective action, autonomous weapons may soon become an unavoidable reality in modern warfare.

The ethical risks of autonomous weapons extend beyond the battlefield—they challenge the fundamental principles of human morality, legal responsibility, and the future of warfare itself. If unchecked, the rise of AI-driven combat systems could lead to a world where war is waged at machine speed, without human conscience or ethical restraint. The decisions made today regarding the regulation and oversight of autonomous weapons will determine whether AI remains a tool for national defense or becomes a destabilizing force that undermines global security and human dignity. The international community must act now to establish clear legal and ethical boundaries before AI-driven warfare spirals beyond human control.

Can There Be Global AI Governance?

The rapid advancement of artificial intelligence has raised significant questions about global AI governance, as nations, corporations, and researchers grapple with the challenges of regulating a technology that transcends borders. AI has the potential to revolutionize industries, enhance global economies, and improve human well-being, but it also poses serious risks, including algorithmic bias, privacy violations, autonomous weapons, and geopolitical instability. The challenge of governing AI is particularly complex because AI does not operate within a single jurisdiction—its development, deployment, and consequences affect nations worldwide. As AI becomes more deeply embedded in critical infrastructure, decision-making, and security systems, the question remains: Can there be a unified global approach to AI governance, or will fragmented national policies lead to technological divides and ethical inconsistencies?

One of the key obstacles to global AI governance is the lack of consensus on ethical standards and regulations. Different countries and political systems have varying perspectives on AI's role in society. Democratic nations tend to prioritize privacy rights, transparency, and individual freedoms, while authoritarian governments often focus on AI for mass surveillance, social control, and national security. The European Union has taken a leadership role in AI regulation through its Artificial Intelligence Act, which categorizes AI systems based on risk levels and imposes strict requirements on high-risk applications, such as biometric surveillance and predictive policing. Meanwhile, the United States has adopted a more market-driven approach, allowing private tech giants like Google, Microsoft, and OpenAI to lead AI development with minimal federal oversight. China, on the other hand, has integrated AI into state-driven initiatives, using it for economic growth, military advancement, and comprehensive digital surveillance. These ideological and regulatory differences make it difficult to establish a unified global framework for AI governance.

Another challenge is the competitive nature of AI development, often described as an AI arms race. Nations and corporations view AI as a strategic asset, leading to reluctance in sharing data, research, and technological breakthroughs with competitors. Countries investing heavily in AI-driven military applications, cybersecurity, and autonomous weapons may resist international regulations that limit their strategic advantages. The lack of trust between global powers complicates efforts to create binding agreements on AI ethics, data sharing, and safety protocols. Without cooperation, there is a risk that AI governance will become a fragmented landscape of conflicting national policies, where some nations implement strict AI regulations while others allow unchecked development.

Despite these challenges, there are growing calls for international AI governance frameworks, similar to those established for nuclear weapons, climate change, and cybersecurity. The United Nations, the OECD, and the European Commission have proposed global AI guidelines that emphasize human rights, accountability, and fairness. Several AI research institutions, including OpenAI and DeepMind, have advocated for collaborative AI safety measures to prevent unintended harms. Some experts propose an AI equivalent of the Geneva Conventions, where nations agree on ethical limits for AI in warfare, surveillance, and human decision-making. While such agreements may not completely eliminate risks, they could set global standards and prevent the worst-case scenarios of AI misuse.

One possible path toward global AI governance is through regional alliances and voluntary cooperation among leading AI powers. The G7 and G20 could play a role in developing shared AI ethics principles, while public-private partnerships between governments and tech companies could help create industry-wide safety standards. AI governance may also require independent regulatory bodies, similar to the International Atomic Energy Agency (IAEA), to monitor AI developments, ensure compliance, and prevent the reckless deployment of dangerous AI technologies.

Ultimately, global AI governance is both a technological and political challenge. If nations fail to establish a cooperative approach, AI could deepen global inequalities, fuel conflicts, and lead to unregulated AI systems that threaten human rights and security. However, if international collaboration prevails, AI governance could ensure that AI remains a tool for human progress rather than a force of division and exploitation. The future of AI regulation will depend on whether nations can overcome competitive rivalries, prioritize ethical considerations, and commit to responsible AI development before the technology outpaces our ability to control it.

Chapter 8
Will AI Replace Human Creativity and Purpose?

The rise of artificial intelligence has led to profound debates about its impact on human creativity and purpose. As AI systems become increasingly sophisticated, they are now capable of generating art, writing literature, composing music, and even designing products—domains once considered the exclusive territory of human imagination. AI-powered models such as GPT-4, DALL·E, and MidJourney have demonstrated the ability to create poetry, paintings, and even film scripts that rival human-made works. This rapid evolution raises existential questions: Will AI eventually replace human creativity? If machines can produce art, music, and literature, what will remain uniquely human? And in a world where AI performs many traditional jobs, will humans struggle to find meaning and purpose? These concerns challenge long-held beliefs about the nature of creativity, innovation, and human self-worth in an AI-driven future.

Creativity has long been considered one of humanity's defining qualities, rooted in emotions, cultural experiences, and individual expression. Unlike machines, humans create not just for functionality but also to express feelings, tell stories, and explore personal and collective struggles. AI, by contrast, generates content by analyzing vast amounts of existing data and predicting patterns, rather than by experiencing emotions or forming original ideas. While AI can mimic artistic styles, replicate existing works, and even "learn" to produce new variations, critics argue that true creativity requires intent, self-awareness, and a deeper connection to human experience—qualities that AI lacks.

However, others believe that AI is not replacing creativity but enhancing it. AI-driven tools enable artists, musicians, and writers to expand their creative capabilities, allowing them to experiment with new styles, generate ideas, and automate tedious aspects of their work. Graphic designers use AI-powered programs to visualize concepts more efficiently, musicians employ AI to assist in composing melodies, and writers integrate AI into brainstorming processes. In this view, AI acts as a collaborative partner, amplifying human creativity rather than replacing it. Instead of viewing AI as a threat, some argue that it should be seen as a new medium for artistic expression, much like photography or digital art once were when they first emerged.

Beyond creativity, AI's growing role in the workforce raises deeper concerns about human purpose in an automated world. Many jobs that once required human intuition and creativity—such as marketing, journalism, and entertainment—are increasingly influenced by AI-driven automation. This shift has sparked fears of a future where AI-driven efficiency reduces human participation in creative industries, leading to job displacement and a crisis of meaning. If AI handles everything from storytelling to composing symphonies, will people struggle to find value in their work? The concern is that AI could transform creativity into a commodity, reducing the deeply personal and introspective aspects of artistic expression to an algorithmic formula.

Yet, human purpose is not solely tied to labor or creativity—it is also defined by relationships, emotions, aspirations, and the quest for meaning. AI may excel at generating content, but it cannot experience joy, heartbreak, or the profound sense of wonder that drives artistic and philosophical exploration. In an AI-driven future, humanity may redefine its sense of purpose, shifting from productivity-based identity to one that prioritizes exploration, ethical responsibility, and deeper human connections. Rather than replacing human creativity, AI could challenge us to redefine what it means to be human, pushing us toward new frontiers of innovation, philosophy, and self-discovery.

The question of whether AI will replace human creativity and purpose remains open-ended. Much depends on how societies choose to integrate AI into cultural and creative fields. If AI is developed and used responsibly, it could serve as a powerful tool for enhancing human expression and exploration rather than diminishing it. The future of creativity and purpose in the AI era will not be determined by technology alone, but by the choices humans make in shaping how AI is used and valued in society.

The Fear of Losing Human Uniqueness

The rapid advancement of artificial intelligence has sparked a profound existential fear: the loss of human uniqueness. As AI systems become increasingly capable—generating art, writing literature, composing music, diagnosing diseases, and even making complex decisions—many wonder whether the qualities that make us distinctly human are being eroded. AI can now replicate tasks that were once thought to require uniquely human intelligence, raising concerns about our role in a future where machines outperform us in areas once considered the pinnacle of human achievement. This fear goes beyond job displacement and automation; it is a deeper anxiety about the essence of humanity, creativity, consciousness, and our sense of purpose in the world.

For centuries, human beings have defined themselves by their intellectual abilities, emotions, creativity, and capacity for moral reasoning. The belief that humans are the only truly self-aware and conscious beings has long set us apart from other forms of intelligence. However, as AI models become more advanced, mimicking human reasoning, generating original works of art, and even engaging in philosophical discussions, the lines between human and artificial intelligence appear to be blurring. If AI can paint like Van Gogh, write poetry like Shakespeare, or compose symphonies with the complexity of Beethoven, what does that mean for our claim to uniqueness? If machines can outperform us in problem-solving, data analysis, and even social interactions, what remains exclusively human?

One of the primary sources of this fear is the redefinition of creativity and intelligence. Historically, intelligence was seen as an innate human trait, shaped by experience, intuition, and emotional depth. AI, however, does not "think" or "feel" in the way humans do; rather, it processes patterns, predicts outcomes, and generates responses based on vast amounts of data. While AI can create stunning visual art or compose beautiful music, it does not experience joy, heartbreak, inspiration, or the thrill of artistic creation. Its outputs are sophisticated but lack the underlying emotional journey that defines human expression. Yet, the growing ability of AI to mimic creativity and intelligence makes many question whether human artistic and intellectual efforts will be devalued or replaced altogether.

Beyond creativity, the fear of losing human uniqueness extends to consciousness and moral decision-making. Humans are capable of deep self-awareness, ethical dilemmas, and subjective experiences that shape our identities. AI, despite its complexity, does not possess subjective experience or moral autonomy—it follows programmed rules and statistical probabilities. However, as AI takes on roles in healthcare, law, governance, and security, making decisions that impact human lives, the concern arises that society may increasingly defer to AI's logic over human judgment, diminishing the value of human wisdom, empathy, and ethical reasoning.

Another dimension of this fear is the potential for humans to become overly dependent on AI, leading to a loss of essential skills and cognitive independence. As AI systems handle everything from driving and cooking to decision-making and emotional support, there is a risk that humans will lose touch with the very qualities that define them, becoming passive participants in a world dictated by machine intelligence. If AI becomes the dominant force in innovation, problem-solving, and social interaction, will future generations still develop the same depth of knowledge, curiosity, and self-reflection that have driven human progress for centuries?

Despite these concerns, human uniqueness is not solely defined by intelligence or productivity. Our ability to dream, imagine, love, grieve, and form meaningful relationships remains beyond the reach of artificial intelligence. AI may simulate human behavior, but it does not experience the richness of existence—the uncertainty, vulnerability, and wonder that come with being alive. The true challenge is not whether AI will replace human uniqueness, but rather how humans will adapt and redefine their role in an AI-driven world. Instead of fearing the loss of uniqueness, societies must embrace the opportunity to enhance human potential, prioritize ethical AI development, and ensure that AI remains a tool for empowerment rather than a replacement for human depth and meaning.

The future of human uniqueness lies not in competing with AI, but in leveraging what makes us irreplaceably human—our ability to feel, connect, and shape the world with purpose and meaning. AI may change the landscape of creativity, work, and intelligence, but it cannot replicate the essence of the human soul. How we choose to coexist with AI will determine whether we feel diminished by its presence or empowered by the new possibilities it brings.

AI-Generated Art, Music, and Literature: Is It Real Creativity?

The emergence of AI-generated art, music, and literature has sparked intense debates about the nature of creativity and whether machines can truly be considered artists, composers, or writers. With AI systems like DALL·E, MidJourney, and Deep Dream generating visually stunning paintings, AIVA and OpenAI's MuseNet composing music, and GPT-4 and Bard producing compelling literature, it is clear that AI can mimic human artistic expression with impressive sophistication. However, does this constitute real creativity, or is it merely an advanced form of pattern recognition and replication? The fundamental question at the heart of this debate is whether creativity is simply a product of data and algorithms, or if it requires something uniquely human—conscious intent, emotions, and personal experiences.

At first glance, AI's ability to generate art, music, and literature may seem like a creative breakthrough. AI models trained on vast datasets of existing works can analyze styles, structures, and thematic patterns to generate original-looking pieces. AI can paint in the style of Van Gogh, compose music that echoes Mozart, or write poetry reminiscent of Shakespeare. These outputs can be aesthetically pleasing and even emotionally evocative, leading many to believe that AI is capable of creativity. However, AI does not create with intention, inspiration, or emotion. Unlike a human artist, who may draw from personal experiences, cultural influences, and deep emotions, AI merely processes data and generates outputs based on probabilistic patterns. The resulting work is not a product of introspection or lived experience, but rather an extrapolation of what has already been done.

Real creativity involves originality, emotional depth, and the ability to break conventions. While AI can combine existing styles in novel ways, it does not truly innovate or challenge artistic norms as human artists do. Throughout history, artistic revolutions have been driven by personal struggles, philosophical insights, and social movements—factors that AI cannot experience. Picasso's Cubism, Beethoven's late symphonies, and Kafka's existential literature were not just technical masterpieces; they were deeply personal expressions of the human condition. AI, lacking self-awareness and personal experience, does not create with the same depth of meaning. It can mimic, refine, and recombine, but it cannot infuse art with the same profound sense of humanity and purpose.

Another key distinction between human and AI creativity is intent and authorship. Human artists create with a purpose—whether to tell a story, express an emotion, critique society, or explore an abstract concept. AI, on the other hand, does not have intent; it generates based on algorithms and prompts given by human users. The human element remains crucial in guiding AI-generated works, as the person behind the prompt still makes artistic choices about what to create, modify, or interpret. This suggests that AI is more of a tool for human creativity rather than an independent artist.

However, AI is changing the creative landscape by offering artists, musicians, and writers new ways to explore and expand their creative processes. Many contemporary creators are embracing AI as a collaborative tool that enhances human creativity rather than replacing it. Musicians use AI-generated compositions as inspiration, visual artists refine AI-generated images into unique pieces, and writers use AI to brainstorm ideas or generate poetic structures that they then refine. In this sense, AI can be seen as an amplifier of human creativity, allowing artists to push boundaries and explore artistic possibilities that might not have been conceivable before.

Despite these advancements, the debate over AI-generated art and authorship continues to raise legal and ethical questions. Who owns an AI-generated painting or a song composed by an algorithm? Can AI-generated works be copyrighted, or does ownership belong to the programmer, the AI system, or the human who provided the prompt? These issues are still unresolved, highlighting the challenges of integrating AI into creative industries while maintaining fair recognition and compensation for human creators.

Ultimately, AI-generated art, music, and literature may be impressive, but it is not "real creativity" in the human sense. Creativity is more than just assembling patterns or generating aesthetically pleasing outputs—it is about meaning, emotional depth, and conscious intent. AI lacks the self-awareness, emotional experience, and existential curiosity that drive human artistic expression. While AI can serve as a powerful creative tool, it does not replace the unique human ability to feel, interpret, and innovate in ways that transcend mere computation. The future of art and creativity in the AI era will depend on how society chooses to integrate these technologies—as replacements for traditional artistry or as tools that enhance and expand human imagination.

The Search for Meaning in an AI-Driven World

The rise of artificial intelligence has fundamentally reshaped how humans interact with technology, work, and even understand their place in the world. As AI continues to automate tasks, generate creative works, and make decisions that were once the sole domain of human intelligence, an existential question arises: what is the role of humanity in an AI-driven world? If machines can outperform humans in logic, efficiency, and even artistic expression, what remains uniquely human? This search for meaning in a world increasingly shaped by AI challenges our deepest philosophical beliefs about work, creativity, relationships, and the purpose of human existence.

For much of human history, work has been central to identity and meaning. People have defined themselves by their professions, their ability to contribute to society, and the value they create through labor. However, with the rapid advancement of AI and automation, many traditional jobs are being displaced or fundamentally altered. AI-driven systems are replacing routine tasks in industries ranging from manufacturing and finance to healthcare and creative arts. Even high-skilled professions like law, medicine, and engineering are seeing a shift where AI assists or even surpasses human expertise in certain areas. This raises an unsettling question: if AI can perform our work more efficiently, what will humans do? The fear of obsolescence challenges the belief that professional achievement is a primary source of meaning in life.

Beyond work, AI's growing capabilities in creativity and decision-making further complicate the human search for purpose. Historically, artistic expression, intellectual inquiry, and innovation have been uniquely human endeavors, fueled by emotion, curiosity, and personal experience. But as AI generates paintings, composes symphonies, and even writes poetry, it forces humanity to reconsider whether creativity alone defines our uniqueness. If AI can produce art that evokes emotion or write stories that inspire, does this diminish the significance of human creativity? Some argue that AI will never truly replicate the human experience, as it lacks consciousness, intent, and emotional depth. Others worry that as AI becomes more integrated into culture, human contributions may be overshadowed, leading to a sense of existential disconnection.

In an AI-driven world, the search for meaning may shift from productivity and creativity to relationships, personal fulfillment, and ethical responsibility. Unlike AI, humans experience love, grief, joy, and the struggle for self-discovery—intangible qualities that machines cannot replicate. AI may assist in many aspects of life, but it cannot replace the depth of human connection, the complexities of moral choices, or the introspective journey of understanding oneself. Rather than competing with AI, humanity may find meaning in areas where machines cannot follow—in relationships, spirituality, philosophy, and the ongoing pursuit of knowledge beyond data-driven logic.

The challenge ahead is ensuring that AI serves as a tool for human enrichment rather than displacement. Ethical AI development should focus on augmenting human potential rather than replacing it. Societies must foster a future where people are encouraged to explore new sources of purpose, from lifelong learning and social impact to creativity and self-reflection. If embraced wisely, AI could free humans from mundane labor, allowing greater focus on personal growth, exploration, and the deeper aspects of existence.

Ultimately, the search for meaning in an AI-driven world will not be about what AI can do, but what humans choose to become. The future of humanity is not defined by the capabilities of machines, but by the values, purpose, and wisdom that people cultivate in an era where AI enhances, rather than diminishes, the human experience.

Can AI Enhance, Rather Than Replace, Human Ingenuity?

The rise of artificial intelligence has led to an ongoing debate about whether AI will replace human ingenuity or enhance it. While some fear that AI's increasing capabilities in creativity, problem-solving, and decision-making will diminish human contributions, others argue that AI can serve as a powerful tool that amplifies human potential rather than rendering it obsolete. Throughout history, technology has often been met with skepticism, yet it has ultimately empowered people to push the boundaries of innovation. AI, when used responsibly, has the potential to enhance human ingenuity by augmenting our cognitive abilities, automating tedious tasks, and opening new frontiers of exploration that were previously unimaginable.

One of the most significant ways AI can enhance human ingenuity is by expanding creative possibilities. In fields like art, music, literature, and design, AI-powered tools help creators experiment with new styles, generate ideas, and push artistic boundaries. AI can analyze patterns in vast datasets of historical art or music and generate unique compositions that human artists can refine and reimagine. For instance, musicians use AI to develop melodies that serve as inspiration, while writers leverage AI-powered language models to brainstorm story ideas. Instead of replacing artists, AI acts as a collaborative partner, enabling them to explore new creative dimensions while retaining their human intuition, emotion, and storytelling abilities.

In science and research, AI accelerates discovery by analyzing complex patterns, processing massive amounts of data, and making connections that might take humans decades to uncover. AI-driven models have already contributed to breakthroughs in fields such as drug discovery, climate modeling, and materials science. For example, AI-powered tools like AlphaFold, developed by DeepMind, have revolutionized protein structure prediction, dramatically speeding up the development of new medical treatments. Scientists can now focus on interpreting AI-generated insights, designing experiments, and applying discoveries in ways that require human ingenuity and ethical reasoning.

Another critical area where AI enhances human capabilities is problem-solving and decision-making. AI algorithms assist professionals in fields like engineering, finance, and law by providing data-driven insights, risk assessments, and predictive analytics. By processing vast amounts of information quickly and efficiently, AI helps experts make more informed decisions while allowing them to focus on the strategic, ethical, and creative aspects of their work. In medicine, AI-powered diagnostic tools assist doctors by analyzing medical images, identifying early signs of diseases, and suggesting treatment options. However, human expertise remains essential, as doctors must interpret AI's findings within the context of patient history, ethical considerations, and emotional intelligence—areas where AI lacks depth.

Beyond individual industries, AI can enhance collaborative problem-solving on a global scale. AI-driven simulations help governments and organizations tackle challenges such as climate change, poverty, and public health crises by analyzing multiple scenarios and suggesting optimal solutions. AI can help researchers model the effects of environmental policies, optimize resource distribution, and even predict potential pandemics. However, these AI-driven insights must still be evaluated by human decision-makers who consider ethical, political, and cultural factors that AI cannot fully comprehend.

Despite these advantages, AI's role in enhancing human ingenuity depends on how it is developed and integrated into society. If AI is designed to replace human creativity, intuition, and problem-solving, it could lead to over-reliance on machines and a loss of essential human skills. However, if AI is used as a collaborative tool, it can empower individuals to explore new ideas, innovate faster, and focus on high-level thinking rather than repetitive tasks.

Ultimately, AI does not possess true ingenuity—it lacks consciousness, emotions, and the intrinsic drive to create. What makes humans unique is not just their ability to generate ideas, but their ability to find meaning, purpose, and ethical direction in their work. AI can enhance human ingenuity by amplifying what people do best: improvising, storytelling, adapting, and envisioning possibilities beyond what data can predict. The key to harnessing AI's potential lies in using it as an enabler of human creativity rather than as a replacement for human thought. The future of innovation will not be defined by AI alone but by how humans and AI collaborate to push the boundaries of what is possible.

Conclusion
The AI Dilemma and the Legacy We Leave

The rise of artificial intelligence has brought humanity to a pivotal moment in history, one filled with both immense potential and profound ethical dilemmas. AI has already transformed industries, revolutionized scientific research, and expanded the boundaries of creativity, but it has also raised fundamental questions about control, human identity, and the balance between progress and responsibility. The AI dilemma is not just about technology—it is about the choices we make today and the legacy we leave for future generations. As AI continues to evolve, we must decide whether it will serve as a force for empowerment and human flourishing or if it will lead to a world where human ingenuity, autonomy, and ethical decision-making are diminished.

At the heart of the AI dilemma is the question of alignment—how can we ensure that AI systems reflect human values and work for the collective good rather than for unchecked corporate, military, or governmental interests? AI is being deployed in everything from healthcare and finance to law enforcement and national security, making decisions that affect millions of lives. The challenge is that AI lacks intrinsic morality, emotions, and ethical reasoning—it operates based on data, probability, and programmed objectives. Without responsible oversight, AI could amplify biases, invade privacy, or even be weaponized in ways that destabilize societies. Ensuring that

AI remains aligned with human ethics, fairness, and accountability will require ongoing regulation, ethical frameworks, and global cooperation.

Another aspect of the AI dilemma is the impact on human identity and purpose. Throughout history, human progress has been driven by creativity, labor, problem-solving, and the search for meaning. With AI increasingly capable of automating tasks, generating creative works, and making complex decisions, there is a growing fear that humans may lose their sense of purpose in an AI-driven world. However, rather than seeing AI as a replacement for human intelligence, we must recognize that it can be a tool for enhancing human potential. AI can free people from mundane tasks, allowing them to focus on innovation, relationships, and deeper existential pursuits. The real challenge is ensuring that AI empowers rather than erodes the uniquely human aspects of creativity, ethics, and emotional intelligence.

The choices we make today about AI governance, ethical development, and societal integration will shape the legacy we leave for future generations. If AI is developed responsibly, it has the potential to solve global challenges, accelerate scientific discoveries, and create a more equitable and interconnected world. However, if left unchecked, AI could lead to unprecedented inequalities, mass surveillance, and ethical blind spots that undermine democracy, human rights, and autonomy. The responsibility lies not just with governments and corporations, but with every individual— researchers, policymakers, artists, and everyday citizens—to advocate for AI that prioritizes human dignity and progress.

Ultimately, AI is not just about technology—it is about humanity's relationship with the future. The legacy we leave will not be determined by AI itself, but by how we choose to wield it. If we approach AI with wisdom, foresight, and ethical integrity, it can be a tool that enhances human civilization rather than diminishes it. The defining question of our time is not whether AI will replace us, but whether we will shape AI in a way that elevates our shared humanity. The future of AI is not just about machines—it is about the values, vision, and responsibility we embrace as we step into the next era of human evolution.

www.ingramcontent.com/pod-product-compliance
Lightning Source LLC
LaVergne TN
LVHW061527070526
838199LV00009B/398